EARTH RESOURCES RESEARCH

Earth Resources Research Ltd is a charitable environmental research agency based in London. It was established in 1973 and is associated with Friends of the Earth, the environmental activist group.

ERR depends for its existence on the generosity of various trusts, foundations and concerned individuals who covenant money to support our research. The organisation employs full-time staff qualified in disciplines ranging from the natural and applied sciences to social sciences and economics, and hence is able to approach each problem or subject area in an interdisciplinary fashion while at the same time being able to call on the specific expertise of its staff and consultants. ERR works by a system of Policy Research Units of which the Social Policy Unit, responsible for the production of this report, is one. Other fields of investigation include Food and Agriculture, Land Use, Energy, Transport, Wildlife and Materials.

Inquiries, suggestions for potential research projects and (of course) offers of financial assistance are welcome.

David Baldock
Executive Director
Earth Resources Research Ltd
40 James Street
London W1

ACKNOWLEDGEMENTS

We should first like to thank Malcolm Peltu, Peter Bennett and David Baldock for the substantial help they gave and the suggestions they made throughout the preparation of this discussion document. Others who read drafts and made valuable contributions were Iann Barron, Barbara Dinham, Steve Hahn, Jenny Popay, Caren Levy and Howard Rush. Special thanks are also due to Caroline Holland who typed the seemingly endless drafts, and to Reg Boorer for the cover design.

Notwithstanding the generous assistance and advice which we received, responsibility for any errors—whether of commission or omission—remains that of the authors.

Colin Hines
Graham Searle
Earth Resources Research
August 1979

Automatic Unemployment
Colin Hines & Graham Searle

First published 1979

Earth Resources Research Ltd
40 James Street
London W1M 5HS

© 1979 Earth Resources Research Ltd

Typeset by Modern Text Typesetting
and printed by Temtex Printing Ltd.

Cover design by Reg Boorer,
FOE Publicity Ltd.

ISBN 0 905966 20 1

THE AUTHORS

Colin Hines has been actively engaged in environmental issues for the last nine years. In 1972 he was a founder-Director of the pressure group, Population Stabilization, and in 1974 was co-author of the ERR report, *Losing Ground*, a critical assessment of British agriculture. Before joining the ERR research staff in 1977 he was food campaigner for Friends of the Earth, and for the past five years has been a part-time lecturer in environmental studies at London's Polytechnic of the South Bank. In 1979 he attended the UN Rome Conference on Agricultural Reform.

Following the publication in April 1978 of *The Chips are Down*, his appraisal of the social implications of microelectronic technology, Hines was invited to be co-organiser of the national conference on "Planning for Automation", which was addressed by many participants in the employment debate including Tony Benn; and since then he has co-ordinated the activities of the discussion groups which emerged from the conference. He is currently completing research for a report on the employment possibilities presented by the utilisation in Britain of presently wasted resources of materials, manpower and derelict land.

Graham Searle was a founder and the first Executive Director of both Friends of the Earth and Earth Resources Research. At FOE he was responsible for the inception of the successful campaigns to ban the importation of whalemeat into the UK and to resist pressure to convert part of the Snowdonia National Park into one of the world's largest open-cast mines. Following this he was invited to assist New Zealand conservationists defend one million acres of the country's native forest from chip and pulp mills; and the arguments marshalled in his book, *Rush to Destruction* (Reed, Wellington, 1975), succeeded in persuading the NZ Government to abandon plans to clear-fell.

Searle was active at both the UN Stockholm Conference on the Human Environment in 1972 and the Rome World Food Conference in 1974; and in 1976 was emissary and rapporteur to international non-governmental organisations participating in the UN Vancouver Conference on Human Settlements. This and another commission in 1977 from the Environment Liaison Centre in Nairobi involved lecture and study tours to a number of developing countries. In 1978, while based in Kenya, he acted as consultant to the UN Habitat Foundation and the UN Environment Programme, before—in May 1979—returning to ERR.

Contents

Introduction

In April 1978 Earth Resources Research published a short discussion paper entitled *The Chips are Down*[1] which dealt with the likely effects of the increased use of microchip technology on employment in Britain. In the time which has elapsed since then there have been a great number of reports, articles, TV documentaries and radio programmes on the subject of silicon chips. The debate which ensued, and which still needs to be engaged, persuaded the former Labour Government and Conservative spokesmen until recently in Opposition to make a number of statements on the subject, and culminated in substantial funds being made available in an attempt to promote the rapid utilisation of microelectronics by British industry.

However, it is clear from their public pronouncements that the major parties—whether in or out of Government—have failed to pay sufficient attention to the likely effects of microprocessors on the structure and the very nature of employment in Britain. Instead the makers of policy have placed their trust in the belief (or at least the claim) that something is bound to turn up: that somehow new jobs will be created by the new technology and that these will compensate for jobs lost.

It is this Micawber-like approach which prompted the publication of this second ERR discussion paper. In it attention is drawn to the likely dimensions of the reduction in traditional employment opportunities which will accompany the revolution in microelectronics, and an attempt is made to give an indication not only of the number but also of the range of jobs which will be lost. While acknowledging the difficulties which beset policy-makers, the paper highlights the inappropriateness of the responses of successive governments to the role of information technology and to its employment implications. Alternative strategies for the alleviation of immediate problems are advanced. It is argued that without a fundamental reappraisal of the whole structure and purpose of employment itself problems of far greater magnitude and social significance will be encountered in the future.

1 The response of government

Support for the Industry

Nineteen seventy-eight was the year in which "chips" came to mean more than the companion to fish on the corner shop's menu. Chips, when they appeared in last year's newspapers, were, more often than not, of silicon rather than potato, and instead of laced with vinegar were etched with minute integrated electronic circuits: chips had come to mean microprocessors and memory stores, the ever smaller and ever more ubiquitous elements of modern computers.[1]

But, as these new proofs of man's ingenuity were rewarded with more column inches in the press and more air time on television and radio, the wonder which they provoked was gradually replaced by a realisation that the undoubted advantages which they bestow are not without attendent problems. The greater use of microchips in offices, supermarkets and industry which had occurred insidiously and almost unnoticed by the public had indeed (in however small a way) begun to fulfill its promise of saving human labour. But it was doing so at a time when the preoccupation of many was to secure and to retain work rather than to surrender it.

Although the previous Government expressed awareness of the possible employment effects of the use of microelectronics, its actual policies were limited to funding the manufacture of chips and encouraging their increased use by industry in an attempt to ensure that Britain remained internationally competitive. In the twelve months up to February 1979, the Labour Government committed nearly £400 millions of financial support to the microelectronics industry.[2] As part of this package, in June 1978, £50 millions was pledged, through the National Enterprise Board, to Inmos, a microelectronics production company.[3] In December 1978 a five-part programme was launched by the Departments of Industry, Employment and Education and Science. It was to cost £100 millions over three years, the money being devoted to publicising the potential of microelectronics; training and retraining workers; reorientating education arrangements; providing direct government support to industry; and gearing public sector purchasing to accommodate microelectronic products.[4] At least up to July 1979, after the Conservative Government had taken office, support for microelectronics was maintained, the most recent development being the instigation at the Central London Polytechnic (with financial support from the £55 million Microprocessor Application Project administered by the Department of Industry) of a programme to provide more than 1,000 engineers, scientists and managers with training in microcomputer systems and their applications.[5]

This policy, as it has evolved in the last year, has followed closely the recommendations of the Advisory Council for Applied Research and Development's report, *The Application of Semi-conductor Technology*, published in September 1978.[6] ACARD (which was established in 1976 to advise the Government of the industrial significance and consequences of scientific and technological advances) set up a working party in June 1978 to look at both the opportunities provided by microelectronics and the effects their application was likely to have. Its report was submitted to the Government in July 1978. The working party, which consisted of industrialists, civil servants and academics, would appear to have had a remarkable impact. Its suggestions have been followed almost in their entirety, and the speed with which the Labour Government pumped large sums of money into the industry seems to demonstrate sympathy with ACARD's view "that a favourable economic climate will be necessary if nationally we are to make the most of the opportunities which semiconductor technology offers."[7] But, while it is possible for a government quickly and easily to make money available to a particular industry, it is very much more difficult for any government to ensure that those displaced by the technology it is promoting are not relegated to the ranks of the unemployed.

This was the theme of much of the media coverage and discussion afforded to microchips in 1978; and, as the year progressed, there emerged what in hindsight might almost appear to have been an orchestrated attempt by the Labour Government and Conservative Opposition to soothe public concern about "technological unemployment". Reassuring but seemingly ill-founded statements were made by the former Prime Minister[8] and by Labour Cabinet ministers including the then Employment Minister, Albert Booth;[9] Secretary of State for Industry, Eric Varley;[10] and the Lord Privy Seal, Lord Peart.[11] But reassurance was not confined to the Government benches: it was similarly to be found in the pronouncements of Conservative spokesmen formerly in Opposition, particularly those of the present Secretary of State for Industry, Sir Keith Joseph.[12]

The argument which was advanced, from whichever side of the House, was largely that, provided Britain adopts the new microelectronic technology as fast as its competitors, jobs created will compensate for jobs lost. There is, however, little evidence to suggest that this will prove to be the case; and even boldly assertive official statements have frequently been obliged to shift to surer ground by emphasising that if the UK does not rapidly expand her use of microelectronics then her competitors will still do so, and the result will be an *even greater* loss in jobs. While the latter is generally agreed, the claim that the new technology will bring sufficient new jobs to replace redundant ones remains much more contentious.

A Thought from the Think Tank

Perhaps the most significant clue to the reasons for the former Cabinet's apparent complacency lies in the contents of one slim, unreferenced paper published by the Central Policy Review Staff — the "Think Tank" — and entitled *Social and Employment Implications of Microelectronics.*[13]

The report's "guardedly optimistic approach" is reflected in its assertion that: "everything will depend on whether job creation matches job reduction . . . we have yet to be convinced that microelectronics will be a major factor for the worse, unless the general prospects for employment make for increased unwillingness to accept technological change."[14]

While the report looked at a number of industries and services, much of its substance (and of the media coverage it received) concentrated on comparisons between recent advances in microelectronics and the introduction some years ago of computers into Civil Service departments. This development had, likě that of silicon chips, brought speculation about job losses, but instead there was an increase in employment in the sections affected, and whatever staff were "freed" by computers were absorbed in new services.

As a basis for a sanguine projection about the likely future balance between job losses and job gains, the example is singularly misleading for two reasons. First, until recent cutbacks, the expenditure increases in the Civil Service were enormous, and themselves permitted significant growth in staff. It is no more than convenient for the Think Tank's thesis that the introduction of the computer coincided with the biggest expansion in the role and functions of government departments in the history of the UK: an expansion, given the attitude to public expenditure of the present Government, which is unlikely to be repeated.

Second, computers did not result in the job losses expected because, when they were first used, their unsuitability for a number of the tasks for which they were purchased actually resulted in an increase in staff requirements. This occurred because — although early computers were advertised and sold on the basis that they would improve industrial and administrative efficiency, consequently allowing staff numbers to be reduced—at the time they were purchased neither the salesmen, the systems builders, nor the actual users fully understood their capabilities. Not only were the huge machines of the 1960s ill-suited to some of the applications for which they were sold, but work styles were changed to suit the needs of the computers and data processing departments, often to the detriment of organisations' efficiency.[15] A whole new servicing industry grew up, with new workers at clerical, technical and managerial levels. In the 1960s and early 70s the combination of inefficient machines and unreliable software systems, which took a long time to be implemented, not infrequently led to unnecessary extra work and to a net increase in staff. It is only now, thanks largely to the low cost computing power of the new generation of microcomputers (but also to the availability of more proven software and improved user understanding of how to get the best out of a computer), that this trend is beginning to be reversed.

The danger of the Think Tank using the experience of the introduction of computers to indicate (if not explicitly to conclude) that fears about expected job losses are ill-founded is that today's situation is quite different from that of ten years ago. Recent technical advances such as the microprocessor, "distributed computing" (in which terminals can be distributed between different branches or sections of an organisation) and better, but far from good, software and systems design, have enabled computers to do what their salesmen had proclaimed them capable of doing a decade earlier. These innovations have meant, for instance, that clerical-level computer jobs that had materialised to perform such tasks as punched card data preparation are now disappearing.

Though the conclusion of the Think Tank report that in the UK Civil Service the employment effect of computers "has been at best to restrain the growth of clerical employment and certainly not to reduce it"[16] might be true, it has not universally been the case. The Australian insurance company, AMP, for instance, has claimed that, without computerisation in the early 1960s it would now be employing about 1,000 more staff.[17] The Civil Service example is of even more doubtful relevance when applied to the introduction of microelectronics, which will affect a far greater range of tasks than those that can be carried out by their bulky predecessors.

The CPRS Report also considered office automation outside the Civil Service, and again concluded that this led to increased productivity but not to staff cuts. This finding was criticised by APEX, the Association of Professional, Executive, Clerical and Computer

Staff, which claimed in its response to the report that it "would have no difficulty in matching each CPRS instance of no job loss through word processors (one application of the new technology) with a case where job losses have occurred."[18] In its opinion "the cases cited by the CPRS, particularly in relation to the office, cannot justify the overall conclusions which it reaches."[19] APEX accused the Think Tank of producing a "seriously deficient analysis" of the social and economic impact of microelectronics. It attacked the report's "bland acceptance" of the "optimistic" view that job losses in traditional industries will at least be compensated for by a growth in employment in new sectors as new products are developed and as the purchasing power released by the anticipated massive increases in industrial productivity finds its way into the economy. The union's most telling criticism was that "The justification for this conclusion in the supporting case studies is virtually non-existent and may lead some observers to conclude that the Report's writers have worked back from its conclusions to find evidence to justify them, rather than reaching them on the basis of an objective study."[20]

It certainly appears that more convincing examples than those supplied to the Labour Government by the Central Policy Review Staff will be required before any government can fairly reassure the electorate that the innovation of microchips will have no profound effect on job availability. (Indeed, in this regard it might prove a significant paradox—or perhaps a Freudian slip—that one social advantage attributed to microprocessors by the Think Tank was that with them "people could obtain from terminals in their homes or in Post Offices up-to-date information about benefit entitlement without the need to visit a Social Security Office.")[21] But, their deficiencies notwithstanding, the conclusions of the Think Tank were clearly accepted by the previous government. The Labour Minister of Employment, Albert Booth, argued that the history of plastics and large commercial computers showed that there was "ample time for the economy to adjust to such changes."[22] In his view, the unions are sufficiently strong to mitigate any hardships that might result from dramatic changes in the job market.

The Department of Employment itself has, thus far, similarly appeared confident that new jobs will materialise. Its own study group, set up in June 1978, would seem to attach great importance to the additional wealth that the introduction of microelectronics is relied on to create. Jonathan Sleigh, leader of the group, has suggested that this wealth will result in an expanded market for new products such as TV games and home computers, leading to a substantial number of new jobs.[23] Sir Keith Joseph, now Secretary of State for Industry in the

Conservative Government, is also optimistic that the threat of "technological unemployment" will be countered by the development of new employment opportunities in new areas.[24]

But such views are not shared by many of the independent analysts who have examined the problem. In a recently published report submitted to the Department of Industry's Computers, Systems and Economic Requirements Board (CSERB), the authors, Iann Barron and Ray Curnow, drew attention to the paucity of new products born of the microelectronics revolution and concluded that the negative labour effect of the new technology "is much higher than the relatively trivial positive labour requirements for, say, electronic TV games."[25] In a similar vein, a recent Arthur D. Little study[26] estimated that, on the most optimistic assumptions, new products could be expected to provide a total of only one million jobs, these to be shared between the USA, France, the FGR and the UK.

Estimates of jobs to be lost run dramatically higher than this; but failure fully to appreciate the likely scale of associated problems is not the only criticism which can fairly be levelled at the former Labour administration (and which, unless there is a fundamental review, will also be applicable to the present Conservative Government). The policy of simply encouraging British industry to employ microchip technology was anyway too narrow in focus. Whatever the potential benefits of silicon chips, merely to encourage their increased use without recognising that they are but one element in the whole field of information technology is likely to militate against the full realisation of whatever advantages could be realised.

The Government fails to grasp IT

Information technology (IT) is a term used to describe the interrelated applications of microelectronics, telecommunications and computing. It is understandable that the mass media, when dealing with information technology, should focus their attention on chips insofar as these are visible objects (which can be photographed), the intricacy of which can be marvelled at and the potential applications of which can be listed. Being essentially tiny computers, microprocessors can be programmed to control particular operations or to solve particular problems. Their programmability makes them extremely flexible, and this, together with their cheapness and small size (computer processing power is now 1,000th of the cost of 15 years ago[27] and a fraction of the size), makes them easy to integrate into a large number of products ranging from watches to spaceships. Malcolm Peltu, an information technology consultant and former editor of *Computer Weekly,* claims that these capabilities make the microprocessor a "Star Trek Enterprise Machine",[28] taking computer power to where no computer power has gone before and leading to the phenomenon termed "distributed computing and processing". Instead of one large central computer processing data and crunching numbers, computer power can be distributed around organisations in the form of "intelligent terminals" and small satellite computers linked—if this is required at all—to the central system. In this way a control centre can be connected, say, to a shop floor terminal and a word processor typewriter in an office.

To make distributed processing work, all these independent devices must be linked into a telecommunications network. A fully automated office, for example, depends on suitable telecommunications facilities linking different offices, and automatically transmitting memos, facsimiles etc. All the other facilities envisaged for what has been termed the "information society" (like electronic mail, electronic funds transfer, data banks, viewdata and online access to data banks) similarly depend on the right kinds of telecommunications.

Peltu feels that the entire Government policy has been distorted by the concentration of reports like that of its Advisory Council for Applied Research and Development merely on silicon chips. It is the convergence of telecommunications, microelectronics and computing into a single information technology which Peltu feels it is vital to grasp. Concentrating on microprocessors alone will not solve or change very much. It is essential also to have far-seeing policies on telecommunications facilities in the UK and Europe. The use of microchips in manufacturing, eg in robots or microprocessor-controlled machine tools, is no more than the further pursuit of an existing trend. When, however, the microprocessor is used as a component in information technology, it becomes an information processor, and starts, for the first time, actually automating the dissemination, retrieval and use of information.

The importance of information technology has been recognised by, among other countries, Japan, France and the USA. If, as seems likely, more advanced, all-digital, voice and communications networks are installed in the USA and Japan before they are in Europe, these countries are likely to acquire a far greater competitive edge than that given merely by being more advanced in the application of silicon chips.[29] This is because such networks would permit them to implement and to use advanced information technology more rapidly and thereby to improve their efficiency by enabling their industries to make better use of microelectronic innovations.

It is thus information technology as a whole, rather than the isolated fields of telecommunications, microprocessors and computers, which is dominating the thinking of large corporations. The biggest contestants in this arena are probably IBM and the telecommunications giant AT&T (known as Ma Bell). IBM has recently acquired a stake in a communications satellite, and AT&T is planning to introduce a data-communications network which would enable all information technology devices to be linked up. As *Business Week* said recently, "Ma Bell is on a collision course with IBM."[30] But the importance of this is that leaders in their own individual fields recognise that the future lies not in the separate development of communications and computers and microchips, but in the convergence of these technologies.

Other companies on the battlefield include Xerox, which actually withdrew from the main computer market some years ago, and Exxon, the multinational oil corporation, which has been gathering together a collection of information technology subsidiaries. In Britain, GEC has recently bought an American office equipment manufacturer and is also heavily involved in Viewdata, while Plessey has set up a special division to use its telecommunications experience to develop products for the office.

In reviewing these developments Peltu concludes that "if the major multi-national companies plus a whole flotilla of smaller, energetic, growing companies have decided to put their eggs in the information technology basket, you can bet your bottom dollar or European Monetary Unit that this is the way technology will be driven unless there is some other force to oppose it."[31]

The first person to emphasise the importance of information technology in Britain was Professor Iann Barron, one of the three founders of Inmos, the microprocessor production company recently established by the National Enterprise Board. Barron and Ray Curnow, a former member of the University of Sussex Science Policy Research Unit, in the report (originally entitled *The Future of Information Technology*) they submitted to the Department of Industry's Computers, Systems and Economic Requirements Board in January 1978[32] claimed that the official attitude to electronics and computing was far too limited and that the Government had failed to understand what was going on: "The developments of the technology mean that electronics, computing and communications need to be seen as interrelated aspects of a more basic information technology. The reduction in cost of this technology means that it will be pervasive, extending throughout commerce and industry . . ."[33] The report went so far as to say that "The use of information technology will directly influence the efficiency of 95 per cent of the economy . . ."[34] The authors called for something like a new government ministry to be set up to deal with the problems likely to arise from the increased use of microelectronics. Government money, the report suggested, should be spent on creating an active programme of investment in an advanced telecommunications system. This would both provide an infra-structure for an information-based society, and create a market for it.

The French Government published, in May 1978, its own study—the Nora-Minc report—which is very similar to that of the Department of Industry's CSERB.[35] (Its publication was delayed until after the election in March 1978, the paper having been presented to President Giscard d'Estaing in January.) This report, like that of Barron and Curnow, talks of massive structural unemployment, with information technology bringing about such important gains in productivity that the internationally competitive sector of the economy will diminish in its social importance. The result would be an economic structure with declining high-employment manufacturing industries and "a fermenting cauldron of small economically viable enterprises on which the responsibility of innovation and the creation of economic wealth in international markets will fall, and on the other hand a mass of socially orientated organisations concerned more with providing employment and cultural or social purposes than with making profit."[36] The social implications of the emergence of an information-based society would be enormous.

2 Unemployment and the effects of microelectronics

Size of the Unemployment Problem

Estimates of the present number of unemployed in the United Kingdom vary from the official figure of 1.46 millions[1] to more than two millions. It is estimated that registered unemployment understates the situation by at least 600,000 (these, in the main, being women who do not register);[2] and official figures do not include people only temporarily taken off the register by such job creation schemes as the Youth Opportunities and the Special Temporary Employment Programmes.[3]

So far, very little unemployment can be attributed to microelectronic technology, and today's jobless total is largely the result of the worldwide economic recession, Britain's uncompetitiveness, rationalisation within industry, and public expenditure cutbacks. When considering possible unemployment in the near future, increases in the workforce due to past population growth must also be taken into account. The high birth rate of the late 1950s and early 1960s means that the 1976 workforce will have swelled by over one million by 1982,[4] and this at a time of dramatic change in the structure of British employment.

By 1985, the Department of Employment estimates, the UK labour force will total 27,638,000, compared with 26,246,000 in 1978.[5] Professor Freeman of the University of Sussex Science Policy Research Unit concludes that to bring down the number of registered unemployed to half a million and to compensate for increases in the size of the workforce the number of available jobs will have to increase by 10 per cent.[6] It is against this background of worsening employment problems that the contribution made by microelectronic technology must be set.

The Changing Structure of the British Workforce

The relatively small increases in unemployment that occured up to the early 1970s masked the basic changes which were taking place in the structure of employment. These took the form of a decline in the numbers of workers in primary sectors such as agriculture and mining, and an increase in the ratio of white collar to manual workers.

Between 1951 and 1977 agriculture lost 688,000 employees, and mining and quarrying lost 517,000. Manufacturing too lost 415,000, while, in the same period, private services such as banking, insurance and scientific services gained an extra 1,878,000 employees, and public services such as health and education gained 1,648,000.[7]

In the second half of the sixties there was also a decline in the proportion of employment in the secondary sectors of manufacturing construction and the utilities. Recently this trend has accelerated. Between June 1973 and June 1976 there were job losses in these sectors of 653,500.[8] The pattern is not peculiar to Britain, and has been repeated throughout Europe.[9]

This process has been termed "de-industrialisation", and so far it appears to have been caused mainly by changes in demand and competition rather than in technology. But it would be wrong to assume that it merely involves a simple transfer from production to services: not all forms of production have lost workers, and nor have all services gained them. Before 1975 some production industries had such a high growth of demand and output that, despite productivity improvements, they increased their labour force. Industries in this category include those concerned with computers, office equipment, packaging, spirit distilling and plastic products. Declining demand and rationalisation, however, have meant job losses in two major service industries: transport and distribution.[10]

Predictions about likely growth in service employment must therefore be treated with caution. As Jay Gershuny has pointed out in his book, *After Industrial Society? The Emerging Self-Service Economy*,[11] the purchase of goods to perform services rather than payment for services themselves is becoming increasingly prevalent. As one commentator has put it, "Where once our service money went to laundries, theatres and railways, it now goes to washing machines, televisions and private automobiles."[12] While such a change obviously benefits manufacturing industry, the net result, with increasing automation in manufacture, is a decline in the number of jobs.

Altogether about two million jobs have disappeared from industry over the last ten years,[13] and, because of the high birth rates of the early sixties, an additional million jobs will have to be created between now and 1981 to keep unemployment figures from rising above their present level.[14] But structural unemployment is not just a matter of numbers. The growing imbalances in the labour market also relate to geographical areas, skill requirements and broad industrial sectors. It has long been predicted by more optimistic forecasters that somehow the service sector will continue to expand and to compensate for the loss of jobs in manufacturing. But these very service sector industries are those which will in the immediate future be most affected by developments in information technology.

Microelectronics and Clerical Work

It is in the office, and to a lesser extent in industries such as wholesale and retail distribution, that the rapid spread of information technology will result in the most dramatic transformations. Word processors, facsimiles, "intelligent copiers" and mini- and microcomputers will form a comprehensive information system, automating much of the production, manipulation, storage and transmission of information—the paper shuffling and rote work—presently done by typists, clerks, administrators and management.

In Britain 57 per cent of the entire workforce is employed in the service industries;[15] and here the information handling activities of postal services and telecommunications, insurance, banking and finance, accounting and legal services, research and development, public administration, wholesale and retail distribution and education will all be greatly affected by automation. In the manufacturing industries it is estimated that 30 per cent of total staff are involved in office work whether managerial, administrative, technical or clerical.[16] A discussion document recently published by the Association of Scientific, Technical and Managerial Staffs (ASTMS) estimated that those occupational areas in this sector that will be most affected by information technology (office work and certain service industries) account for about 45 per cent of all employment in the United Kingdom.[17]

The impetus for the rapid introduction of office automation is expected to come from a desire to increase the relatively low productivity of office workers. A US survey[18] showed that in 1974 the average factory worker was backed by $25,000 (£12,500) of capital investment compared with $2,000 (£1,000) for the average office worker. (Comparable figures for the UK are put at £5,000 and £500 respectively.)[19] In the USA office productivity rose a mere four per cent between 1960 and 1970 compared with a rise of 83 per cent for manual workers over the same period.[20] Recent advances in information technology are expected to achieve substantial increases in productivity by virtue of the reduction in unit costs of storage, transmission and access to information they allow.

Future office automation is likely to proceed by two stages. At present each piece of office equipment, such as a typewriter, copier, calculator or telex machine, is designed for its one task and is an isolated unit; and, at first, more sophisticated job-specific devices, like word processors and improved facsimile transmitters, will continue to be introduced into the office in a piecemeal fashion. But later, integrated office information systems will be developed in which each device will be able to perform a number of tasks and all will be linked together in a single office information and communication system, which itself will require a considerable reorganisation of office work. The specialised devices being introduced into offices today are generally capable of being integrated into such a total system when at some future date more comprehensive office automation is required.

Currently most organisations are at the first stage, with word processors being used in more and more offices. the number currently installed in Europe is estimated to be about 100,000 compared with perhaps 350-400,000 in the USA,[21] where their use is expected to double by 1981. There are more than 7,000 word processors in the UK,[22] and Olivetti estimates that the UK market will grow by 30-40 per cent in 1978-79.[23]

A word processor in its simplest form can be no more than an electric typewriter equipped with a visual display unit (VDU), a memory controlled by a mini- or microcomputer, and printing facilities. The image of what is "typed" into the memory (not onto paper) is displayed on the VDU, thus ensuring that the information can be checked before being printed or transmitted. The machine can indent, centre, justify margins, and type over errors. Redrafts can be edited, and standard sentences, paragraphs, letters and address lists can be stored and later recalled and displayed on the VDU by keying in their reference numbers. A "floppy disc" memory can store over 100 A4 pages.[24]

The efficiency of a word processor depends on the work for which it is used. In a mail order company handling vast numbers of standard letters, efficiency could improve by 400-500 per cent.[25] In a more typical office with a mixture of short, non-standard letters, lengthy documents and pro formas, efficiency could improve by 200-250 per cent[26] (and these figures are based on the use of "first generation" equipment and so doubtless understate the potential increases in efficiency possible once misunderstandings and misuses are overcome and more sophisticated machines become available). While a very fast conventional typist can type 70 words per minute, and a conventional automatic-memory typewriter can print at 150 wpm, a word processor connected to the new Siemens laser printer, marketed by ICL, "prints"—though at a lower quality—at 2,000 lines per minute;[27] and the standard high quality printers used by most word processors manage 2,7000 words per minute.[28] Logica, the systems development and consultancy firm, claims that one such word processor can do the work of 3½ to 5 typists on traditional typewriters.[29] With prices as low as £3,000 it is likely that there will be a rapid increase in their use.

But, since word processors are essentially general purpose computers, they can be used to handle payrolls, cash flow, standard and personnel records and manpower planning and also to monitor and improve management productivity. Their effect will not be limited to the replacement of typists. Two recent reports from Europe give some indication of their potential impact. The giant electrical firm, Siemens, has suggested in an internal report[30] that, in the FGR, by 1990, 40 per cent of office work will be carried out by computerised equipment; and Siemens should be in a position to know since it is a large diversified company which manfactures the very equipment which will be required. Similarly the major study of the impact of information technology on the French economy, the Nora-Minc report,[31] has calculated that, over the next ten years, modern computing technology in banking could reduce staff by 30 per cent. Losses of the same magnitude were suggested for the French insurance industry.

Word processors with and without visual displays are now being used by the larger UK-based companies, for example Unilever and Shell. They are mostly of the "stand alone" arrangement, with VDU, keyboard, memory and printer all combined in a desk-like unit. The next development will be to have several keyboard and display units sharing common storage and printing facilities, thereby making maximum use of the equipment. Eventually word processors will be able to be linked into an organisation's central computer giving them access to its power and memory store and allowing information to be transferred between word processors via the computer.

When enough word processors have been installed to make intercommunication between them worthwhile, their impact will be still greater. The first step will be the use of intercommunication to replace memoranda, filing and inter-office copying within single buildings. This will be followed by telecommunications links between offices throughout the world, which will constitute a system of electronic mail. In many cases it is already cheaper to store information electronically than to use paper and filing cabinets, and to transmit information through the telephone system rather than to use the postal service. Now, at IBM and Xerox, the development of internal company communications systems has reached the commercial exploitation stage.[32]

In the USA the Yankee Group of consultants has estimated that by 1982 two thirds of the 500 biggest companies will have internal electronic mail.[33] It has been estimated that the US business communications market will be worth $61 billions by 1980, and $100 billions by 1985;[34] and IBM is cooperating with the European company, Comsat, to develop US-European satellite communications for business purposes.[35] Though at present in the UK the use of electronic mail *between* companies is prohibited, its use within companies is nevertheless potentially significant. Mail from companies accounts for 70 per cent of all mail, and a large part of this is internal to the enterprises.[36] Logica has developed a word processing system which would allow companies to progress towards an electronic mail system, and Unilever and BP are already users.[37]

Another specific example of the present effects of the introduction of word processors in the UK is provided by Bradford Council, which has reduced its Jacob Wells office staff from 44 to 22 with the introduction of nine word processors. The result has been a 19 per cent increase in productivity, and an estimated annual saving of £58-59,000. The Provident Financial Group in Bradford has, while increasing its workload, similarly reduced (by natural wastage) its full time staff from 27 to 17, and part time staff from 13 to three. The British Standards Institution has cut the number of its secretaries and typists by a third. The CEGB has reduced the number of its "girls" from over 50 to 26. National Coal Board Western Area has installed word processing on a pilot basis and has solved its staffing problems by natural wastage, reducing staff from 20 to 14.[38] Other British employers who have installed word processors include local authorities, HMSO, the Post Office, area Electricity and Gas Boards, ICI, Esso, Pilkingtons and the Automobile Association.

These seemingly minor examples within the service sector could in fact herald substantial job losses not only here but in all sections of the economy. A large proportion of the working population, perhaps 45 per cent,[39] have jobs (like order entry and processing, accounts and stock control) which are primarily concerned with information in some form or other. It has been estimated that less than 10 per cent of employees working in manufacturing are now directly involved in the process of production itself.[40] The traditional industrial classification therefore gives no real inkling of the number of information workers there are in jobs which cut across this classification, such as those of secretaries, managers and supervisors, all of whom work with information. Nevertheless, for information workers in general, the ASTMS has forecast that 2.6 millions will lose their jobs by 1985, and that by 1991 the figure will have risen to 3.9 millions.[41]

Within what is normally termed the service sector, the jobs of civil servants, postmen, librarians and newspaper workers will all be changed by the use of electronic information systems. Although this will result in increased efficiency, it will also mean higher levels of unemployment. This has already occurred in the newspaper industry; concern is being expressed by threatened workers in television; and the two largest employers in the UK, the Civil Service and the Post Office, could prove to be affected even more greatly by the changing pattern of employment.

The Association of Scientific Technical and Managerial Staff's research into the banking and insurance sector has estimated that jobs here will fall from 1.1 million to 600,000.[42] The British insurance company, Friends Provident, is already developing its own internal services by transacting insurance business with brokers through a nationwide network of display terminals, which also provide for the composition and printing of policy documents and the automatic handling of premium payments.[43] This "instant policy" system has, they claim, virtually eliminated all paper work from what was a notoriously paper-bound process. It used to take a minimum of three weeks to produce even a straightforward policy from the customer's proposal form, whereas with the new system a policy can be issued in three minutes. The Services Manager of Friends Provident anticipates staff savings of 40 per cent, which will pay for the cost of installing the system.[44]

Thus the introduction of new technology into the office will not stop at the replacement of some secretarial and typing jobs by individual word processors. (These tasks anyway only account for about nine per cent of all office based occupations: other strictly clerical jobs make up 45 per cent of office work.)[45] According to a report commissioned by the National Enterprise Board,[46] office automation will concern everyone whose job involves the handling of information, since it will gradually replace the desk, the typewriter and the filing cabinet by an electronic substitute, a workstation which will be able to perform automatically many currently manual tasks.

In principle, workstations will be able to handle almost any task involving the storage, processing, processing manipulation and transformation of information. This will affect office workers at the clerical level since they are concerned with the transformation of information from its original to its stored form and with its communication to others. Office workers at the executive level will also be affected since they are concerned with assimilating existing information, processing and manipulating it, and generating new material. They in turn often have personal assistants, acting as a link between the executive and the sources and destinations of information.

To one particular group within the labour force this is of profound significance. The importance of office work to women is illustrated by the fact that in 1977, 33.7 per cent of all working women were in secretarial and clerical jobs compared with 7.5 per cent of men.[47] Although unemployment among clerical workers has traditionally been lower than for unskilled manual workers, over the past few years this pattern has been changing. Between June 1975 and June 1978 unemployment among clerical and related workers grew by 68 per cent, compared with a growth in unemployment among manual workers of 32 per cent, and among all workers of 33 per cent.[48]

In the view of APEX, a trade union with over 50 per cent of its membership women, "Whether the improvement (in productivity) results in greater unemployment will depend on the attitudes of government, employers and trade unions."[49] APEX is concerned in that it feels that women are usually considered as a "soft option" for cutting jobs because they are often second income earners, and because they tend not to register as unemployed and so do not swell the official unemployment figures. To counter this it points out that about 30 per cent of working women with children are the sole household earner, that married women with second incomes keep many families of low paid men out of poverty, and that the freedom that employment opportunities give to women is fundamental to the achievement of full equality between the sexes.

APEX has estimated that if, as they think likely, word processors are introduced and used effectively in one fifth of all UK offices by 1983, there could be a reduction in office jobs of roughly a quarter of a million.[50] They anticipate a substantially reduced number of typing and secretarial jobs, of clerks and of document and letter authors. The pressure to expand the use of word processors could be greater in the public sector than in the private. Public spending constraints could make the installation of a shared facility word processor very attractive if, as APEX claims, if would do the work of one typist and hence pay for itself in one or two years.[51] In Central London, where wages and associated employment costs are higher, it could pay for itself in less time.

The necessity of dealing with an increasing workload, and the relatively easy internal spread of information possible with information technology, could make these office developments seem still more desirable. In the private sector, large corporations are experimenting with the technology, and APEX expects small companies like solicitors, estate agents and small manufacturing firms, where trades union organisation is weak and there is less effective resistance to redundancies, also to be affected.

Finally there remains a further issue to be considered when changes in office organisation and operations are discussed. In the trade there is what is already described as an old joke about the microelectronics firm that became so successful it had to move into smaller premises. If the demand for office space were to fall significantly, this could have a considerable impact on overall land values since it is the price of land for office use which sets the pace. While a drop in land prices would be welcome if it reduced property speculation, it might also pose problems for the 50 per cent of householders who are home owners, as well as for insurance and pension schemes that have invested in land for the purpose of securing adequate returns for their clients. One pension fund manager[52] has already declared that the uncertainties posed by rapid technological changes in the next 10 years, particularly in the field of telecommunications, have led him to a preference for investing in shopping centres, rather than in office accommodation.

Microelectronics and the Industrial Sector

Though in the short term it might prove to be clerical workers who will experience the greatest number of job losses due to technological change, manufacturing industry will also be affected. Clive Jenkins and Barrie Sherman of the ASTMS, looking at 21 industries providing 13.6 million jobs, have, with the help of the industries' own forecasts, predicted that job losses in these industries will total 1.8 millions in 15 to 20 years time.[53] This is largely because microprocessors have widespread application in both machinery construction and the replacement of mechanical or electromechanical control devices.

Looking less at job loss, a report by the National Electronics Council[54] which stressed the importance of maintaining international competitiveness for Britain's future economic well-being concluded that microprocessors would provide many new opportunities for using computers in manufacturing. They listed the industries they thought most suitable for automation as metal and plastic fabrication; instrument engineering, electrical engineering; shipbuilding and marine engineering; vehicles; electronic components and assembly; office machinery and computing; aircraft; and printing and publishing.

According to the ASTMS, one industry they missed was textiles, which has responded to international competition by modernising, and has increasingly introduced microprocessors into textile machinery and applied computer-based control systems in textile manufacture.[55] "For example," cites the ASTMS, "Carrington Viyella have opened a new £6 million spinning mill at Atherton, Greater Manchester." The mill is the first to be built in the area for more than 50 years and will produce competitively priced supplies of yarn for the company's household textiles. "This is being achieved through the use of modern highly capital intensive equipment, which will be operated seven days a week, 24 hours a day, using a complex five shift system. The new mill replaces three former Carrington plants which had an area of 45,000 square metres and a combined labour force of 435 people. The new mill has an area of 8,500 square metres and will employ only 95 people."[56] As the *Financial Times* commented, "it may well be that spinning will only survive in other parts of Lancashire if similar economies of operation can be achieved by other companies."[57]

An equally dramatic example of the employment effects of microelectronics is the loss of jobs resulting from the Post Office's changeover in its telephone exchange equipment from the electro-magnetic Strowger-Cross Bar type to the all-electronic System X. This new system is being developed jointly by the Post Office and its main suppliers—Plessey, GEC, and Standard Telephones and Cables (the British subsidiary of the US multinational ITT)—and will make many jobs redundant. The Managing Director of Standard Telephones and Cables, Mr K. G. Corfield, has explained that the switch from the existing antiquated system requiring large "metal bashing" factories to System X lines will transform the manufacturing process into "almost that of a laboratory, eliminating the dirt, drudgery and physical work of current manufacturing with its stamping, pressing, turning, milling, liquid soldering and labour intensive assembly."[58] He has also warned that the all-electronic System X "if properly implemented" would, during the 1980's eliminate the jobs of 90 per cent of the workers currently employed on the production of TXE4, the semi-electronic system which is the first stage in the transition to an all-electronic telephone network for Britain. It will also affect those servicing the equipment. "The impact on our people will be dramatic and, as is usually the case, it will probably be with us physically before we have made the necessary psychological and philosophical adjustments."[59] For every hundred employees required in 1975 by the Strowger-Cross Bar system, only 40 were needed in 1977 for TXE4, and by 1985 System X will require only four.[60]

The speed with which redundancies can arrive is well-illustrated by the American experience. Western Electric, the manufacturing arm of American Telephone and Telegraph which supplies the majority of telephone systems in North America, reduced its direct labour force from 39,200 in 1970 to 19,000 in 1976. It expects this to be down to 17,400 by 1980.[61] AT&T is retiring electromechanical exchanges early simply because electronic exchanges save so much labour in manufacturing, installation and maintenance. Western Electric have estimated that with the new system there will be a 75 per cent reduction in the need for labour in fault-finding, maintenance, repairs and installation work.[62]

Apart from its application in telephone systems, microelectronics also plays an increasingly important role in the development of robots and other automatic handling systems. As their television commercials proclaim, one of Fiat's production lines in Italy is already fully "manned" by robots; and some European car manufacturers have introduced programmable robots into car-body fabrication lines for spot-welding tasks. Both flexibility of production and quality of the product are improved; repetitive, tedious and unpleasant tasks are eliminated; and productivity is increased.[63]

Fiat's new robogate welding line allows the output of different models to match demand precisely. The line is controlled by computer, and, although it costs 30 per cent more than a conventional line, it only needs 25 instead of 125 people to man it. While for the moment it has said there will be no job loss, Fiat has the opportunity to cut manning costs by £500,000 a year.[64]

Volkswagen designs (and sells) its own robots, which are used for spot welding and handling body panels between presses. They can be rebuilt and reprogrammed, and, in theory, three robots can replace ten men on a two-shift system.[65] As the ASTMS has pointed out,[66] VW produces twice British Leyland's declared target with only 80 per cent of Leyland's labour force.

Volvo now has an automatic 10-station body welding line with 29 robots working at full production rate at its Torslanda plant near Gothenburg, Sweden. According to the ASTMS, this line was built at a cost of £3.5 millions and has replaced three manual jig and one manual free-spot spot-welding lines, which were difficult to man efficiently because of high absenteeism and labour turnover on this hard and tedious work. The new line has freed 70 men, 35 on each shift, for "more agreeable work."[67]

The United States vehicle manufacturing industry intends to invest so heavily in labour-saving equipment over the next few years that 128,000 auto-workers (over 18 per cent of the total production workers in the American industry) at General Motors, Fords, Chryslers and American Motors will lose their jobs by 1985.[68]

In Britain panel pressing operations in one car manufacturer's press-shop have employed automated loading and unloading systems and transfer machines, with the effect that the production rate has almost doubled while the manning level has dropped from 12 to two operators plus one extra maintenance worker.[69] Fords plan to introduce new microelectronic equipment as modules within a range of mechanical operations, disc storage devices for data accumulation, and terminal units for inter-office communication.[70] Enots Limited of Lichfield have reduced their workforce from 850 to 650 by using automated machine tools, group technology cells (involving the rearrangement of machine tools into groups to accommodate the machining requirements of similarly shaped components) and a minicomputer for order processing and stock control. Eight automatic lathes can now be handled by just one operator, whereas previously each required its own. The company claims that their new system has given them the flexibility to respond to market demand, and has resulted in the sort of stability and security of (surviving) employment which was impossible to achieve under the old system of one operator per machine.[71] At the Castle Bromwich plant of Processed Steel Fisher a new paint shop now boasts a spray line costing £24 millions which not only greatly increases the automation of the process itself but also has a recognition system to identify which of six different body shapes is to be sprayed and (by means of a code strip on the body itself) which colour is to be used.[72] Elsewhere robots have also been introduced in die-casting operations with an average productivity increase of over 35 per cent. The 32 workers who had previously operated one line were reduced to 26 (including maintenance men), and output was substantially increased.[73]

But, of course, automation is not an entirely new phenomenon. Computers already control industrial process production in petrochemicals, iron, steel, glass, paper and cement; and, in some other industries with production runs of 250,000 or more, it has long been economic to build transfer machines by which objects, all of the same size and correctly positioned, can be moved through various fixed manufacturing and assembly operations. Where microprocessors will have their big impact is in those industries with production runs previously too small to make automation economically feasible. Because microprocessors can be reprogrammed they grant robots increased flexibility and they have substantially lowered costs.

Most robots work by using a microprocessor to control the recording and reproduction of the actions of a human operator. The operator physically guides the robot through its tasks, and the "teaching schedule" is recorded on a non-volatile memory (which ensures that there is no loss of memory during power failures or when the system is switched off for a long period). When the robot memory is played back the robot duplicates exactly the actions of the operative as many times as required.

An even more sophisticated development is the (still experimental) mechanical assembler system devised by IBM. In this a machine can be programmed to perform many different tasks without having to be "taught" them by a worker.

But it is Japan which has taken the lead in the research and development of the fully automated factory. Prototype unmanned factories have been designed, one of them to manufacture 2,000 different machinery items in lot sizes of up to 25 pieces and to assemble them into 50 different products.[74] Automatic operations include forging, welding, machining and painting, as well as the replacement of tools and the self-diagnosis of machine failure and repair, all achieved by a hierarchy of individual workstation micro-computers, inter-cell minicomputer control, and overall control by a larger, central computer. It has even been estimated that, with a control crew of only 10, a fully automated factory could produce the equivalent of a conventional factory employing 700.[75]

However, job losses result not only from the automation of the production process by the use of microprocessors and from the increasing use of information processing machinery containing micro-electronic components. A further development affecting employment is the reduction made possible by microelectronics in the number of components within products. Nowadays, for instance, a single silicon chip in an electronic sewing machine can replace 350 standard parts.[76]

A smaller number of components not only results in job losses for those manufacturing and assembling them (an electronic telex machine, for example, can be assembled in 11 hours compared with the 75 hours needed to assemble a mechanical one[77]), but also means that fewer people are needed to move, store and service machine parts. With less than 10 per cent of employees now working directly in a productive process,[78] the decrease in the number of components has serious implications for the indirect production workers involved.

As a recent ASTMS report has observed: "It is this substitution of electronic integrated circuits for electromechanical components which has led Philips, the world's largest electrical manufacturing company, employing some 425,000 people world-wide, mainly on light assembly work, to estimate that, even allowing for three per cent per annum real increase in turnover for the next 10 years, it will still be 56 per cent overmanned. The implication is that Philips could shed over half of its world-wide force during the next decade.[79]

The implications for the workforce are clear. "The Dutch trade union, NVV," the ASTMS report continues, "recently gained access to a report produced by Philips' personnel and industrial relations department, which outlined the company's plans to cut its workforce in the Netherlands by 20,000 to 65,000 over the next ten years, a 23½ per cent reduction. Philips has already reduced its Dutch workforce over the last few years by natural wastage, replacing only half of those who have retired or left the company."

Products in which the number of components employed is being progressively reduced include clocks, white goods (like washing machines and cookers), office machinery and cars; and increased standardisation using fewer components and computer-aided design techniques will result in fewer design staff being required. But perhaps the most telling example of staff reductions is in the manufacture and assembly of colour televisions. In Japan the number of integrated circuits has doubled, the number of transistors has been halved, and there has been an 80 per cent reduction in the number of other components. The top seven manufacturers cut their labour forces by almost 50 per cent between 1972 and 1976 while increasing the output of sets by 25 per cent, improving their reliability and quality, and reducing servicing and running costs.[80]

In Britain, Thorn Electrical Industries, faced with such competition, have redesigned their television products, introduced more integrated circuits and cut down the number of components. In some areas expected growth in the colour TV market will mean that the labour force will be maintained, but there have been heavy redundancies among assembly workers.[81] In July 1978, more than 2,000 jobs were lost at Thorn's largest factory in Bradford,[82] and some 200 redundant women were retrained to perform clerical duties. But, with the increasing use in and around Bradford of word processors, the jobs they have subsequently secured cannot be considered safe. The local ASTMS official has estimated that some 12,000 clerical, secretarial and administrative jobs will disappear from the area in the next four years.[83]

Finally in a recent report[84] it has been shown that computer control of components and stock handling linked to output requirements will lead to the "optimally efficient" allocation of labour for these tasks, which itself can be expected to result in more redundancies.

Even those who argue that microelectronics will not cause the number of jobless to increase agree that there will be "dislocation" of workers with particular skills. Microelectronics in the manufacturing sector will herald the demise of a number of skilled jobs. A survey[85] carried out under the auspices of the Manpower Services Commission revealed that while many major manufacturers currently face shortages of skilled workers in certain geographical and specialised areas, their long-term requirements for skilled manpower are dramatically lower than their immediate needs. The overall conclusion was that relatively large British companies are planning reductions of up to 30 per cent in their labour force over the next 10 years. These major UK manufacturers foresee a profound polarisation in their labour requirements, with a modest increase in highly qualified technicians, a relatively small workforce of unskilled or semi-skilled personnel and few if any conventionally skilled workers.

It is not only those involved in manufacturing who will be affected. Self-diagnosing machinery will also reduce the need for maintenance skills.

To take an example, the Philips PW 1400 sequential X-ray fluorescent spectrometer is a highly advanced piece of equipment controlled by a microprocessor which takes over 90 per cent of what, with earlier machines, was the operator's job. The software in the machine provides self-diagnosis of faults and can relay this information over a telephone line to a distant service engineer. The immediate benefit is that the service engineer, who anyway needs less intensive training because there are fewer parts, arrives with exactly the right tools for servicing.[86] As the ASTMS has reported,[87] the machine tool manufacturers, Gidding and Lewis-Fraser, have already introduced a remote diagnostic service operated over telephone lines from a fully equipped central base at its Arbroath headquarters. Experienced personnel, using the customer's control equipment cathode ray tube display as a "shop-talk" communication device to augment voice contact by telephone, can guide the user's maintenance man through the most comprehensive diagnostic procedures. With a more powerful microprocessor, fully automatic servicing will be possible, probably under only the supervision of a service engineer at a distant base.

Thus will control over many industrial processes increasingly be concentrated in the hands of a relatively small number of highly paid technicians and professionals. The discretion and job control at present enjoyed by both blue and white collar workers during their careers will be expropriated by control systems and computer-aided or automated design and production techniques.[88] A skilled worker's knowledge will disappear into computer memories and commonly his tasks will be performed by microprocessor-controlled equipment.

For those retaining their jobs in capital-intensive work places, high-cost equipment is likely to dictate an increase in the tempo of work and in shiftwork. There is a danger that, in considering the large scale implications of changes in the nature of employment, such effects on a personal level will be ignored. While Dr J. M. Harrington of the TUC Centenary Institute of Occupational Health has recently dismissed as exaggerated some of the more alarmist claims that shiftwork is damaging to health,[89] a survey in the FGR[90] has demonstrated that the incidence of stomach and intestinal ulcers among those working a rotating shift was eight times that in other workers; their divorce rate was 50 per cent greater; and the juvenile delinquency rate of their children was 80 per cent higher. There are similar examples in Britain.[91]

But—problems of remaining in a restyled workforce notwithstanding

—it is still the lack of employment which is likely to have, at least in the short term, the most damaging and demoralising social effect. As Marie Jahoda of the University of Sussex Science Policy Research Unit has pointed out,[92] employment serves a number of purposes other than providing income. It gives workers a time structure, contact with people outside the family, a definition of personal status and identity, a link with goals other than those of the individual, and the enforcement of activity.

Furthermore, while little research has been conducted, there has been seen to be a high correlation between unemployment, mortality rates and disease in all age groups within the UK and the USA.[93] Indeed it was claimed in a recent television documentary that, between 1972 and 1976, when unemployment in the UK rose by three per cent, 54,000 deaths were attributable to diseases linked to the condition of unemployment.[94] However our society eventually comes to terms with the apportionment of less work, in the immediate future as unemployment rises these problems will be magnified.

3 Methods of reducing unemployment

Government Job Creation Schemes

The realisation that high unemployment would be more than a brief and transient phenomenon has been slow to dawn on decision makers in the UK. As late as September 1976 the former Chancellor, Dennis Healey, claimed that unemployment would "peak before the end of this year" and would "fall throughout the next".[1] Even when, in December 1976, the then Prime Minister promised that to secure the IMF's support for sterling the Government would introduce "tough new economic measures that will increase unemployment during the next year",[2] the apparent assumption was still that the days of high unemployment would soon pass.

When they were first devised in 1975, therefore, the Labour Government's job creation schemes to be administered by the Manpower Services Commission were planned to be short term. Only when awareness grew of the longer term nature of unemployment in Britain were the programmes stepped up. By 1978 the budgetary allocation to them had risen to £530 millions (just £50 millions short of the combined figure for the three previous years[3]) out of a total MSC budget in that year of £693 millions. The Temporary Employment Subsidy was originally planned to run for two years. At the end of a programme costing £347 millions and designed to keep 408,000 people from being redundant, employers faced with laying off 10 or more workers were promised £20 a week for a year for every job they kept (a doubling of the assistance given when the scheme started in 1975).[4] The Job Release Scheme, an official euphemism for early retirement, also, under Labour, became semi-permanent, and, like the Temporary Employment Subsidy, was invoked country-wide whereas in the beginning it only applied to development areas.[5]

Of greatest concern to the Manpower Services Commission has been youth unemployment. When the earliest intervention measures were devised the difficulties and the scale of the school leaver problem were underestimated. People born in the baby boom of the first half of the 1960s are now entering the job market. In 1973 3.7 millions reached the age of 16 and began looking for work; by 1977 this number had grown to 4.2 millions; and the figure will rise to a peak of 4.4

millions around 1980. It will be 1988 before the number of 16 year-olds falls back to the 1977 level.[6]

In the twelve months up to September 1979 the Manpower Services Commission was committed to providing places for 234,000 young people between the ages of 16 and 18 in its Youth Opportunities Programmes; and a further 25,000 places were to be made available for older age groups under the Special Temporary Employment Programme.[7] The 16 to 19 year-old group already constitutes more than 30 per cent of total unemployment,[8] and the proportion is still rising. Amongst ethnic minorities the increase in youth unemployment has been estimated to be four times that amongst whites,[9] and young unemployed blacks were therefore to be given some sort of priority training under the youth opportunities scheme. It was intended (though now the position is not so clear) that twenty "outreach officers" in the careers service would have as their main job that of working with immigrants and organisations representing minority groups.[10]

It has been claimed[11] that the Manpower Services Commission has approached youth unemployment on the assumption that the greatest handicap of young people coming onto the job market is their lack of skills and work experience. These the Youth Opportunities Programme attempts to provide. But such an approach ignores the fundamental questions of whether the young people now being trained will actually be offered jobs at the end of their training period, and of how still more long term employment opportunities might be provided. As one critic put it: "The programme, like most of the (then) Government's economic and social policies, appears as no more than another ill-considered response to a perceived emergency." It was intended, in his view, merely to demonstrate that something was being done, and it obscured the issue of mass unemployment by suggesting that it had something to do with "training" and "skills": "meanwhile resources are directed to train people to do jobs that are not available and to gain experience of work they will never be employed to do."[12]

In spite of such criticisms it has been estimated that in Spring 1979 unemployment in the UK would have stood at nearly 7.3 per cent if it had not been for these special employment and training schemes.[13] But, by the time of the May 1979 General Election, it was equally apparent that, unless the system generated a substantial increase in the number of permanent jobs, the spectacular success which was achieved by the earlier programmes in finding long term jobs for a high percentage of participants would be difficult to repeat. Even if such success were maintained it might only be so at the expense of non-participants in such schemes. The Manpower Services Commission had itself accepted that by giving young people as a whole "a competitive edge", its programmes could "affect adversely other age groups".[14] So too could they adversely affect members of the same age group by granting a minority preferential access to the labour market at the expense of other young people not participating in them.

But such arguments about what should and might have been have recently had to be considerably revised. It is now extremely unlikely that the Manpower Services Commission will prove to be as effective an instrument of job creation in the immediate future as it was in the past. Since the Conservatives gained office and introduced their first Budget on 12 June 1979 it has become clear that a radically different approach to employment provision is to be pursued by government, one in which the stimulation of private industry and the encouragement of entrepreneurship are to be relied on to reduce unemployment levels.

Though the Budget of Sir Geoffrey Howe did not result in the discontinuance of any individual employment support item, special employment measures were cut back. Cuts in the present year's allocations in this field totalled more than £170 millions, of which £110 millions was to come from the Manpower Services Commission.[15]

The Special Temporary Employment Programme had both its budget and the scope of its operations (formerly it was intended to provide 30,000-35,000 jobs by March 1980) considerably reduced. The reduction in available funds was of £42.2 millions; and the new jobs target is 12,000-14,000 jobs by March 1980. The programme is to be restricted to special development areas, development areas and inner cities.

Similarly the funds available to the Youth Opportunities Programme were cut by £25.2 millions. The target of finding 100-120,000 jobs by March 1980 was retained, but less expensive employment opportunities were to be sought, and young people were to stay in the scheme for shorter periods. £22.3 millions was cut from the MSC's Training Opportunities Scheme (mainly by reducing clerical and commercial training); the Industry Directorate was required to reduce its support of industry training boards and other such bodies by £9.8 millions; and support for unemployed people moving to other areas where work is available was cut by £2.9 millions.

But, though that was the extent of the immediate cuts announced in the Budget, it was not the full extent of proposed reductions. According to two letters from the Secretary of State for Employment to the Chairman of the MSC and an internal document prepared by the Commission (copies of which were leaked to the *Morning Star*) the Government has asked the MSC to cut its expenditure by £300-£450 millions in the three years from 1980.[16] Cuts of up to 20 per cent of the MSC's 25,000 employees were to accompany cuts in actual programmes.

"Progressive reductions" in the planned number of filled places in the Youth Opportunities Programme were to be designed to achieve savings of 15-20 per cent. The Training Opportunities Programme placements were similarly to be reduced from 70,000 to 40,000. At worst this scheme would have to be halved with an end to all clerical training and "considerable reductions in commercial, management and other training,"[17] this at a time when local government expenditure on further education was also facing sizeable cuts. According to the internal document, the Special Temporary Employment Programme would have to be phased out entirely by 1981.

Far from denying the existence of these plans, the Government reacted to their disclosure by ordering an inquiry into leaks of confidential documents to the press.[18] It would seem prudent, therefore, to anticipate cuts in the job creation activities of the MSC in excess of those announced in the June 1979 Budget. The full effect of these changes cannot yet be measured; but, in the short term at least, unemployment in the UK is likely not only to rise (as it would in all likelihood anyway have done) but to rise at a considerably faster rate.

The Situation Abroad

However much they might be aggravated by the advent of micro-electronic technology, the problems of structural unemployment in general and of youth unemployment in particular are not unique to Britain. It has been claimed that in the EEC there are now nearly four times as many young people out of work as there were two years ago.[19] In France more than 35 per cent of the unemployed are under 25 years of age; in the Netherlands the proportion is over 40 per cent; and in Belgium just under 35 per cent.[20] One estimate puts the figure for anticipated unemployment in the EEC at 12 millions by 1990,[21] an important contributing factor being an above average increase in the population of working age which is not expected to be reversed until after that date.

Even the seemingly impregnable economy of Japan is confronted by problems of unemployment as the number of its jobless rises. Despite the fact that fewer than two per cent are officially unemployed, key sectors of the economy are facing substantial redundancies. A third of Japan's textiles workforce, for example, is being laid off. The position is similar in shipbuilding; and the iron and steel industry is working at well below capacity with the result that mills are closing down.[22] The

President of the Japan Automobile Workers' Union expressed fears recently that the still booming motor car industry will also be required to contract over the next few years.[23] More and more private manufacturing companies are falling heavily into debt to banks. Japanese companies' tradition of employing people for life has resulted in four million workers turning up to work each day in spite of there being nothing for them to do.[24] Massive and growing underemployment places a sizable financial burden on the companies, and the fear is that employers will price themselves out of the market.

The United Nations International Labour Office Bureau of Statistics and Special Studies surveyed 15 European countries, Australia, Canada, Japan, New Zealand and the United States and found that, in spite of their job creation programmes providing 12,600 jobs daily, "1,900 people were added to these countries' army of unemployed every single day in 1977. The job outlook for young people under 25 deteriorated practically everywhere."[25]

In addition to the problem of youth unemployment the survey showed that the ranks of women job seekers increased much faster than those of men, and that growing numbers of dismissed older workers joined the hard-core unemployed.

The Organisation for Economic Co-operation and Development has drawn attention to three of the most serious consequences of prolonged unemployment among young people: the overall reduction of a society's resources of skills; a growing alienation of the young from the political and social order that condemns them to unemployment; and what has been termed the "ratchet" effect, whereby the longer unemployment persists, the more likely it is to pervade the following generation.[26]

Some of the efforts to tackle youth unemployment in other countries are similar to those devised in Britain. In Australia 85,000 young people have been assisted by the Special Youth Employment Training Programme, which subsidises employers for supplying six months employment and training to young people aged 15 to 24. In Denmark 17,000 employment and training opportunities were created for young people in the first six months of 1978. It is planned to encourage voluntary early retirement for workers over 60, and it is estimated that for every 1,000 older workers who leave, 750 job openings will be created for young people. In France the National Youth Employment Pact has been renewed and extended. This provides incentives for small and medium size enterprises and craftsmen to employ first job seekers and is expected to benefit 270,000 young people. In Italy financial inducements are offered to employers in industry to hire young persons from 15 to 29 years of age. The same scheme is applied in the agricultural sector, especially for the farming of waste land, and young people are also employed in public schemes to carry out socially useful work.[27]

In the United States about three-quarters of all current expenditures for employment and training are directed to the young, with the 1977 Summer Employment Program for Young People having provided a million federally subsidised jobs for disadvantaged young people aged 14 to 21 in state and local government and in private non-profit bodies.[28] In a report of relevance to planners in the UK and entitled *The Job Generation Process*[29] David Birch has examined how jobs are created and lost in the USA. His research showed that two thirds of all new jobs came from firms less than five years old. The middle size or large companies did not generate new jobs; nor did firms with a long history of stability. Yet these are the companies to which government in the USA has traditionally turned as the most accessible and congenial in the job generating process.

The report, which consulted records covering more than 80 per cent of all private sector employment in the USA, concluded: "The job-generating firm tends to be dynamic (or unstable, depending on your viewpoint) . . . It tends to be young. In short, the firms that can and do generate the most jobs are the ones that are most difficult to reach through conventional policy initiatives."[30] In the opinion of its author, nothing much can be done to prevent the decline in the numbers of jobs in the USA, now running at eight per cent a year.

This conclusion, in the particular context of worldwide youth employment, would seem to be borne out by the ILO. Internationally, they comment, "no remarkable dent in youth unemployment has been made."[31] Like Britain's Manpower Services Commission's latest schemes — the Youth Opportunities Programme and Special Temporary Employment Programme — other national programmes tend to concentrate on short term job provision and retraining. Regrettably, the very immediacy of employment problems seems to preclude adequate consideration of further changes likely to be wrought by the revolution in microelectronics. There would appear in the countries surveyed to be no real idea of how to provide sufficient paid employment for the whole workforce or equitably to reduce the amount of work done per person.

4 Production for social needs

Planning Employment

While there are many different opinions of what to do about them, it is now generally accepted that Britain's unemployment problems are of a long term, structural nature, rather than of the sort that, like the Cheshire cat, will fade away leaving only a smile at the next upturn in world trade.

It is indeed grimmer than that. It seems inevitable that the number of unemployed will grow, particularly as increased use is made of microelectronics in primary industry, manufacturing and services. If such estimates as five million unemployed in the UK by 1990[1] are not to become real, a large number of new jobs must be found, and (for it appears to be a necessity) the paid work that is available will need to be shared more evenly.

Recently many have argued that unemployment could be substantially reduced by a major shift in the economy in the direction of a more adequate provision of unmet social needs.[2] Such commentators have pointed to the absurdity of high unemployment existing at a time when there is modern plant and equipment underused, when Britain's public transport systems are affected by spares shortages, hospitals lack basic equipment, and over a million homes are substandard. They claim that the employment potential is enormous, but that conventional market mechanisms and associated corporate policy are unable to realise it. It is therefore necessary, they argue, to restructure production in such a way that economic activity is devoted primarily to the production of products and services to meet social needs.

Within such a framework, rising energy and raw materials costs, and growing concern about the adverse effects of today's industrial system on the environment, also dictate a need to develop different technologies and new kinds of products which will minimise environmental damage and be frugal in their use of scarce resources. A recent report from the Batelle Institute in Geneva[3] has suggested that substantial employment and a more rational use of resources could come from reversing the present trend in the manufacturing sector which has led to the ever-greater production of short-life, disposable products which cannot be reconditioned, recycled or repaired. Its authors argue that if products were designed to increase their potential for maintenance, re-use and recycling considerable real savings and benefits would accrue. For instance, if a car were designed with a 20 year lifetime, instead of for 10 years, the energy consumption per car year would be reduced by 72 per cent and the labour requirement increased by 56 per cent per car year.[4] As it is, such advantages are not realised, and it is not only the useful life of products which is shortening: the same is true of the machinery which makes the products. In the car industry the rate of obsolescence of plant and equipment has increased dramatically in the last decade or more.[5] But, however easy it might be to identify cases in which the provision of socially beneficial goods and services is eminently desirable, actually to achieve such a goal is far from straightforward.

The Role of the Workers

Perhaps the first workers clearly to articulate the importance of production for social needs were those employed by the Lucas Aerospace Company, 70 per cent of the product range of which is defence-orientated. Here the (then 14,000[6]) employees formed a Combine Committee representing as a lay body all the manual and staff workers in the 13 sites within Lucas Aerospace and Defence Systems. The committee was set up in the late 1960s when it was realised that automation and technological innovation, far from bringing about a shorter working week and more leisure time, were in fact causing redundancies for increasing numbers of both manual and staff employees. In early 1974, following the energy crisis, the Combine Committee began to analyse critically the company's policies and to identify alternative products which could keep Lucas employees in their jobs.

However, the products suggested in their "Corporate Plan"[7] (subtitled "An alternative contingency strategy to recession and redundancies") were not chosen merely because they would provide work. The members of the Combine Committee were also concerned about "the appalling gap which now exists between that which technology could provide for society and that which it actually does provide".[8] As an example they cited the considerable resources and technological sophistication devoted to the production of Concorde at a time when there were not enough simple heating systems to prevent old age pensioners dying from hypothermia.

The 1,200-page Combine Corporate Plan provided detailed proposals for the manufacture of socially useful products using existing facilities and the skills of the workforce. New production lines were to be phased in as the demand for other production activities declined, thus avoiding the usual redundancies. A balance was struck between long and short term projects, some products being designed for use in Britain and some in developing nations. Certain lines would require a large capital investment, while others could be produced almost immediately. Products ranged from components for low energy housing (like solar heating systems and heat pumps) to large scale wind generators for community heating schemes, and from auxiliary ("fail-safe") braking systems for cars, coaches and trains to a hybrid road/rail vehicle. Already the Lucas workers manufacture heart pacemakers and kidney machines; and their concern both for job-protection and socially-beneficial employment was evident when they joined with unions and the local Trades Council in opposing the company's plans to sell off its kidney machine division to a large international monopoly. Their argument was simply put: "We regard it as scandalous that people are dying for want of a kidney machine, when those who could be making them are actually facing the prospect of redundancy."[9]

The Labour Government expressed support for the Lucas workers in public statements, but in practice did nothing to assist them. Indeed eventually the Department of Industry, ignoring the Combine Committee's proposals, awarded Lucas a grant of £8 millions to continue with its rationalisation programme[10] (which, in 1978 included the closure—with the loss of 1,450 jobs—of its Victor works in Liverpool caused by the switch to electronic production systems[11]). Now, after many years of refusing to meet the Combine, the company has agreed to begin discussions with it, though in their public statements Lucas management has indicated that it remains unlikely that the Committee's proposals will gain acceptance.[12]

Nevertheless, the potential implictions of the proposals of the Lucas Committee (some of which the company claims earlier to have considered), and those of others who have actively participated in the debate, are considerable. In the field of energy alone, there is—at least in the short term—great scope for fuel conservation and job provision.

In their study, *A Low Energy Strategy for the United Kingdom,*[13] Gerald Leach and his colleagues at the International Institute for Environment and Development recently concluded that with appropriate government policies, and without austerity measures, enormous investments which would otherwise go to energy supply could be released for other purposes: "The emphasis on (energy) conservation would create a great diversity of jobs, unskilled as well as skilled, in thousands of factories and workshops across the country—in sharp contrast to the specialised, centralised and limited job opportunities implied by conventional supply-expansion energy forecasts and policies."[14]

Workers in the power engineering industry are campaigning for the recommissioning of small, urban and suburban power stations to run on a combined heat and power basis in which the "waste" heat from cooling towers is put to direct use in district heating schemes.[15] Such CHP stations have the advantage of not being restricted to one fuel. Though coal is the most likely choice for most stations (since Britain has large reserves which can be burned efficiently using the latest techniques in fluidised bed combustion) municipal wastes can also be used: one third of Rome has been heated since 1964 by the pyrolysis of domestic refuse.[16] Various estimates of the job-creation capability of combined heat and power systems have been advanced[17] and these, and the other benefits claimed for the system,[18] merit careful scrutiny. While as yet there is little official support for CHP installations in the UK,[19] these are used for district heating in a number of European cities including Berlin, Hamburg, Munich, Moscow, Warsaw and Paris, and are widely employed in Denmark and Sweden.[20] If suitable institutional and private buildings in the UK were to be heated by such district schemes many jobs could be created in the power engineering and construction industries, and at the same time the overall efficiency of energy use could be considerably increased[21] with significant savings in fossil fuels.

Though the need for the electricity which they could supply must itself be questioned (since there is no shortage of electricity in the UK and since only a small part of our energy demand is for electrical energy) wind power systems could similarly result in fossil fuel savings and work creation in the engineering and aerospace industries. Wave power (while at present the costs involved might make this a less attractive venture) could likewise provide this double benefit. In both cases precise estimates of associated job creation are fraught with difficulties, but shop stewards at Vickers Barrow have already proposed diversification into wave power as part of their campaign to protect jobs.[22]

Turning from energy supply to energy conservation—as the IIED study[23] suggests we should—the UK Building Research Establishment estimates that a national building insulation programme could save 15 per cent of our current primary energy requirements.[24] To date, Government backing for such a programme has been modest: £250 millions has been committed to energy conservation in order to insulate public buildings, schools and two million council houses. Different cost estimates have been advanced for the insulation of Britain's housing stock. Gerald Leach and Frederic Romig have concluded that the average cost per dwelling would be £200-£250 for permanent, high-standard insulation,[25] while David Elliott, working on the assumption that some 19 million houses would be involved, has suggested that costs might total only £1,800 millions and could generate 120,000 job years of direct work, as well as indirect employment, for example in the materials industry.[26] While the latter figures both for costs and jobs appear over-optimistic, work generation in a comprehensive insulation programme could clearly have real short term significance.

Finally, and perhaps most important, the rapid implementation of solar collector systems for domestic and industrial space and water heating could create a great number of jobs in construction, engineering and the materials supply industry. Realisation of their full potential for space heating will depend on advances being made in the technology and economics of heat storage; but the United Kingdom section of the International Solar Energy Society has estimated that 14 per cent of Britain's energy could come from the sun,[27] and the House of Commons Select Committee on Science and Technology estimates that by the year 2000 Britain could obtain more energy from solar power than it does from nuclear power today.[28]

In the USA a study by the California Employment Development Department has claimed that *per unit energy* a solar programme would create 6.6 times as many jobs as an equivalent nuclear programme; and another by the Council on Economic Priorities concluded that a conservation and solar programme would, for the same energy output and at considerably less cost, provide 5.4 times as as many jobs as a nuclear one.[29] Though, in a physical as well as a metaphorical sense, the UK is not so well placed as most parts of the USA, it is worth noting that the production of solar equipment is seen in the USA as a means of combating the unemployment crisis in the US aerospace industry; and Leonard Woodcock, President of United Auto-Workers, has, with this in mind, called for "a solar unit for every American home".[30] In California alone it has been calculated that solar power could create 376,000 new jobs between 1981 and 1990: 137,000 directly (including 27,000 in solar collector manufacturing) and 82,000 in installation.[31]

In the UK several local authorities are already investigating the practicalities of the increased use of solar power: Wandsworth, Lambeth, Leeds, Hull and Milton Keynes are experimenting with solar and "low energy" council housing projects. If solar power were to form an important part of UK energy policy, jobs would be created not only in the building industry, but also in the manufacturing and associated industries producing glass, plastic, aluminium and steel.

In this respect an interesting suggestion is to be found in the Lucas

Combine Committee's Corporate Plan.[32] This contains designs for a range of solar collecting equipment (based on work already done in producing such components) and for a low energy house which could be constructed on a self-build basis. Students on the Communications Design degree course at the North East London Polytechnic are now compiling an instruction manual[33] which would allow people without any particular skills themselves to construct the dwellings; and, the Lucas Combine Committee feels, adequate government funding could enable the unemployed to build their own houses in areas of acute housing shortage.

Drawing together all of these potential benefits, a study published by the Centre for Alternative Industrial and Technological Systems[34] (which was established in 1978 in conjunction with the Lucas Combine Committee) has estimated that if a national alternative energy and energy conservation programme were initiated it could result in major increases in employment in several sectors of the economy. The study suggests that the overall programme could, by the year 2000, supply about 26 per cent of Britain's current primary energy at a capital cost of just over £21 billions, and, directly and indirectly, could create 1,520,000 man years (about 30,000 job lifetimes) of work. In contrast, argues its author, the current nuclear programme will on the most optimistic assumptions supply a maximum of 28 per cent of Britain's primary energy needs, will cost something of the order of £35 billions, and will create a maximum of 660,000 man years of work.[35]

In the opinion of the present authors the CAITS estimates of the employment benefits of the preferred programme are greatly over-stated, particularly with regard to the assumed combined energy contribution of solar, wind, wave and tidal systems which is nearly four times the "official" estimate.[36] The capital costs and multiplier effects of the systems discussed are also in need of review. But this sort of study, with the benefit of greater sophistication in its approach (for instance, notice must be taken of choices to be made, say, between group solar and district heating systems: the use of both cannot be maximised simultaneously) could prove extremely useful. This is true not least when consideration is given to the question of whether the UK should place greater dependence on nuclear power—a question raised once more by the recent IIED study[37] which concluded that, given a commitment to conservation and the development of suitable technology, Britain could improve her overall standard of living without any increase in energy consumption.

Arguments such as these, and the Lucas Combine Committee's Corporate Plan in particular, have created interest throughout the world, especially in Sweden, the FGR and the United States, where conversion of military to civilian production is a major issue. In Washington, for instance, the Corporate Plan was used to support the Defense Economic Adjustment Bill[38] of Senators George McGovern and Charles Mathias, which was concerned with defence cuts and the corresponding transfer of resources and jobs to the production of socially useful products. It is the Lucas Combine Committee's opinion that, by showing such a change of emphasis is feasible, their Plan strengthens moves for peace. They feel that, in the past, discussion of defence spending has been too greatly influenced by the issue of employment in the industries concerned. By reducing the impact of this argument they consider that it will become possible for defence spending and project development to be decided on the criterion of national security alone, and they contrast this, for example, with the recent B-1 bomber project in California, where the jobs involved were the major issue.[39]

The Lucas initiative was the first of its kind and was regarded as significant enough to be nominated for the 1979 Nobel Peace Prize.[40] In its wake other groups of workers including those at Vickers, BAC and those in power engineering, machine tools and car industries are themselves endeavouring to conduct critical analyses of corporate policies and practices and to put forward their own alternative production proposals.

However, such initiatives can prove unwelcome to management, and workers are aware that their acceptance, or at least fair and thorough appraisal, is in practice likely to depend on the degree of support provided by other trades unions and groups of workers, especially those in closely related industries. In the UK trades unions have considerable political power, and it has already been suggested,[41] for instance, that members of the National Union of Public Employees could insist that the placing of orders for more kidney machines or other medical equipment of the kind proposed in the Lucas plans be included as part of the normal wage-bargaining process. It is possible that similar action could be initiated by the National Union of Railwaymen and the Transport and General Workers Union with the road/rail vehicle, or by car workers with the auxiliary braking system.[42]

To be effective such support would have to be widespread, and it can be anticipated that trades councils will play an important role in any combined effort. In the past these have brought together workers from a range of industries and sectors, and have been a focal point for community campaigns requiring trade union support. Trades councils represent the labour movement in various local institutions, and have recently coordinated many of the campaigns against government public expenditure cuts. Though these have tended mainly to involve public sector workers, as jobs in the private sector continue to disappear and unemployment increases, trades councils could progress from merely organising protests by the community and public and private sector workers to proposing and gaining support for constructive plans for alternative employment.[43] It must be expected— especially as increased use is made of the labour-saving potential of microelectronics—that attempts to insist that socially beneficial use is made of presently wasted resources of unemployed people, empty factories and idle capacity will become increasingly common.

The Role of the Community

Clearly, if they are to have a significant political impact, proposals for the retention of existing jobs or the provision of alternative work to counter redundancies will need not only to have the support of the workforce itself but also of the community at large.

In some cases such support has already been achieved. In Sunderland in 1977 opposition to the closure of a Plessey factory rallied round the slogan, "These are the town's jobs". In the same year on Tyneside local support was mobilised for the campaign by Parsons workers to win the Drax B order, and now the next step is the development of a plan to secure other work whereby jobs will be retained when the Drax B boilermaking is completed.[44] In both cases the community saw that they, as well as the workers directly involved, would suffer from a loss of employment. It is recognised that if the economic base of a community is allowed to crumble, more jobs will be lost indirectly; and attempts by the local community to prevent large scale job losses and closures are bound to become a more common feature of efforts to resist redundancies.

In the opinion of some observers, labour-shedding by large companies will mean that small firms and workers' cooperatives will, in the future, be increasingly substantial providers of employment. One group which has worked with local authorities in establishing small firms is URBED (Urban and Economic Development Limited), a non-profit research and consulting group which specialises in obtaining funds for practical schemes to assist in the revival of run-down local economies. Part of their work involves feasibility studies to test the economic viability of proposals made by people wanting to start small enterprises; and the group's approach is that there is no shortage of opportunities for new firms since there are always gaps in the market that are too small or too unconventional to interest large companies.

Initiatives can come from a local community rather than from individuals, and this was the case, for example, in the London Borough of Lewisham. Here, the Telegraph Hill Neighbourhood Council suggested that in order to provide training and employment opportunities in the area, a clothing factory and workshop facilities should be established. Lewisham Council commissioned URBED to carry out a feasibility study, and a multi-disciplinary team was assembled. Weekly programme meetings were held with representatives from the Neighbourhood Council and local authority, and the team's findings[45] persuaded the local authority to support the project in the period before it became self-sufficient. URBED concluded that, "Given the right combination of well organised and practical voluntary groups and a sympathetic local authority, it is possible to set up viable employment-generating projects in inner city conditions."[46] The clothing cooperative, "Telegraph Textiles", will be situated in converted warehouses, along with a creche, canteen and five small workshop units. The funding for this conversion came from the Docklands Rolling Programme; and for the first two years the salaries of the workers, as well as the funding for a training scheme, will be met by the Manpower Services Commission's Enterprise Workshop Scheme (a sub-section of the Special Temporary Employment Programme which now seems likely to be axed). The URBED study indicated that after the two year period of support the firm should achieve commercial viability.

People keen to set up a small business but who lack previous experience could, unless the scheme is discontinued as part of the Conservative cutbacks,[47] be helped by a three month preparatory course which is one of the Manpower Services Commission's experiments to assist small enterprises. The course is sponsored by the Training Services Division of the MSC, and its purpose is to enable participants to formulate their business plans fully prior to total financial commitment. It begins with an intensive lecture week encompassing marketing, financial planning, business administration and government legislation, and is followed by three months of individual work relating this range of information to the participant's business plan. Participants meet once a week to assess progress, and jointly identify objectives to be attained. The course forms part of the Training Opportunities Programme, each participant being eligible to a training allowance of £30-£40 per week and a marketing research budget of £500. The programme, like the enterprises it promotes, is small scale, but its contribution is not insignificant. According to the report of one course with 15 participants, for an expenditure of approximately £14,000, the Manpower Services Commission can expect to claim a "return" of 52 new jobs, including partners, cooperators and employees.[48]

Judy Bartlett, the Employment Development Officer for Lewisham's Voluntary Action, considers that the power and resources local authorities possess make them the best vehicle for generating employment at a local level.[49] Examples of these powers include the 1972 Local Government Act Section 137 which enables local authorities to spend up to a 2p rate to benefit the borough or its inhabitants for any purpose not authorised under any other act; and the Inner Urban Area Act which allows certain local authorities to provide money to help with the costs of site preparation, and even to grant an initial rent free period in the letting of factories. But there are clearly limits to the ability of local authorities to provide work. The funds available to them and employment levels in their areas are inevitably affected by outside decisions, whether by large companies or by national government (witness the expenditure cuts of £440 millions for local government and water authorities in England and Wales announced in the June 1979 Budget[50] and the cuts in regional development aid to industry announced subsequently[51]).

At present local authorities' attempts to increase employment tend to be restricted to the passive provision of sites and factories and re-zoning for industrial use. Lewisham Council, for example, also endeavours to co-ordinate the various bodies concerned with education, training and retraining in order to bring about a closer relationship between their activities and the skills required by industry and commerce. Representatives from the employers, educational establishments and the local authority meet in an "Employment Forum" set up by the Council. It is hoped that new firms, particularly those employing labour-intensive methods, will be encouraged to move into the borough in sufficient numbers to offset any decline in jobs, and that existing firms will be persuaded to expand locally.

But, valuable though this might be, a less reactive and more positive approach is advocated by Bartlett. First, in her opinion, in order to plan for labour shedding in both private and public sectors, local authorities should conduct detailed studies of trends in the private firms and public organisations located in their districts. If this were supported by an examination of manufacturing and office activity in general it could enable the local authority to obtain some idea of what new enterprises might be expected (and encouraged) to materialise. Tameside, for example, has commissioned a study of the likely effects of micro-electronics on the labour demands of the firms that operate within their area;[52] and Hertfordshire County Council Planning Department has already begun to monitor the effects of microelectronics on Structure Planning.[53] Predictive researches might also include consideration of employment trends in the public sector, such as in nationalised industries, hospitals, schools and central government departments. In this way local authorities would be able to arrive at some assessment of the number and types of jobs which are likely to be available locally in ten years time, and to do what they can within their limited powers and resources to minimise problems stemming from redundancies.

While they should not be exaggerated in the context of the magnitude of anticipated unemployment, some opportunities do exist for relatively small-scale job creation. It is possible, even with present financial stringencies, for public money to be used productively and at the same time to meet real needs for employment and for goods and services. Appropriately exercised community control over projects and imaginative planning can also do something to ensure that locally accumulated capital is retained and reinvested in the locality or spent in other desirable ways. But it nevertheless remains extremely unlikely that the entrepreneurship which it was hoped would be stimulated by the first Conservative Budget, and the efforts of local authorities and communities (which to some extent have been circumscribed by that Budget), will succeed in holding UK unemployment at present levels, let alone in reducing it.

5 Work sharing and job creation

The Reorganisation of Available Work

At present in the UK there are at least 1.46 million men and women unemployed. By 1985 the workforce is expected to have grown by nearly 1.4 millions.[1] Technological unemployment (not least that brought by microchips) is anticipated, and there is a gloomy outlook for international trade. There are simply insufficient jobs to go round, and the situation will worsen. Unless the maintenance of a larger pool of wholly unemployed is to become a permanent feature of the British economy, some form of more equitable work sharing will need to be invoked; and already a number of proposals—including the 35-hour week, overtime bans, early retirement, job sharing, longer holidays, sabbaticals, more further and high education, and retraining—have been advanced.

The first of these to receive serious consideration was the 35-hour week. This and the likely effect of microprocessors on employment were two topics which dominated the 1978 TUC Conference, and in the future the shorter working week will become an increasingly important element in wage bargaining. Already British Post Office engineers have taken industrial action not merely to protest against the introduction of new technology, but also to attempt to minimise anticipated redundancies by the establishment of a 35-hour working week. The eventual settlement inaugurated a 37½ hour weekly work period with no increase in overtime.[2] Many engineers now work a four day week or, to provide the Post Office with the staff cover it requires, a nine-day fortnight with longer shifts. The settlement was to be at no extra cost to the Post Office, so in this example, while jobs will be saved, no more will be created.

Estimates of the number of jobs that might be preserved (and could be created) by a shorter working week remain a matter of contention. The April 1978 edition of the *Department of Employment Gazette* put them at between 100,000 and 500,000, whereas John Hughes of the Trade Union Research Unit, Ruskin College, has quoted figures as high as 750,000.[3] One seemingly intractible problem is that of progressively making good the job losses associated with the introduction of new technologies. Jenkins and Sherman of the ASTMS conclude[4] that the relationship between the reduction in hours worked and the new jobs created cannot be more than two to one at best: for every two per cent reduction in hours, only one per cent more jobs would be saved or created. Thus the 16 per cent unemployment rate these commentators consider a possibility would require to be countered by a reduction in hours to a 27½ hour working week. But the question is one not only of how many hours, but also of how many days might be worked.

Jenkins and Sherman are critical of the present concentration on the 5-day, 35-hour week since they feel that it is too limited in its effect on employment and will not do enough to improve the welfare of workers. A one hour cut per day will still mean coping with rush hours while not allowing enough of an increase in time off to develop other activities. This sort of change would also require a four-shift system for many processes, which would be accompanied by other disadvantages. Instead they urge a reduction in the number of weekly or monthly trips to work. In their opinion, a 4-day week, on the basis of an 8-hour day, is more likely to necessitate the employment of extra workers than is a reduction of one hour per day, since the latter can be accommodated more easily by shift changes. This approach would also have the advantage of providing a substantial increase in leisure on a regular basis. While they are aware of the problems attendant on such a seemingly simple solution (and themselves suggest that longer holidays and sabbaticals have a role to play) Jenkins and Sherman conclude that if it alone is to ensure equitable work-sharing the working week would, by the year 2000, have to become a three times 8-hour day.[5]

But, in the short term, even more problematical than the numbers involved is the question of paying for the shorter week. The unions want for their members the same pay as was received for longer hours.[6] The CBI, in its report, *Britain means Business,*[7] has argued against this on the grounds that it is inflationary. It is claimed that unit costs would rise, making British products even more uncompetitive, with the likely result being a further 100,000 redundancies. The CBI also fears that the 35-hour week would prove a back door method of increasing the amount of overtime, and asserts that "employers must be more willing than hitherto to act together on issues of common concern — in particular the pressures for a shorter working week."[8]

It seems certain that for the 35-hour week to save jobs there would indeed have to be a substantial cut in overtime. In the past, actual hours worked have fallen more slowly than the length of the basic working week,[9] and overtime unquestionably plays a major part in bringing a large number of people's pay packets to a level they consider acceptable. For any government, the difficulties of successfully pursuing a pay policy which limits wage increases while at the same time restricts overtime appear almost insurmountable. (Perhaps the least problematical—but still real—question is whether, in the process of reducing the hours worked by the existing workforce, "new" shifts would have to be paid more to compensate for working what would become "unsocial" hours.)

Nevertheless efforts are being made in Holland, Italy and Belgium to get a 36-hour week written into future wage contracts,[10] and some delegates at an EEC meeting in Brussels, which brought together European employment ministers, unions and employers, argued in 1978 that the EEC should make a shorter working week mandatory.[11] Since then the European Metal Workers Federation has produced a Charter calling for a shorter working week, and the European Trades Union Confederation, recognising that unemployment is the major problem facing it, has pressed the EEC Commission to issue directives on a shorter working week and the limitation of overtime.[12] However, at the 1978 meeting Britain's representative from the Ministry of Employment, John Grant, stated what remains the British Government's view. Though some overtime worked might be excessive, Britain would not want overtime restriction or a shorter working week imposed by law. Rather, the length of the working week should be left as something to be settled by unions and employers in the normal process of collective bargaining.[13]

Like the 35-hour week, the economics of early retirement have lately been debated in the British press. The idea that they should retire on their present pensions, rather than achieving higher incomes by remaining in the workforce, is unlikely to appeal to many middle-aged employees. An additional factor has now been added by the June 1979 Budget, in which officially retired people had the levels at which their income becomes taxable raised substantially, thus permitting them to keep more of the money which many commonly earn in part-time employment. This will probably encourage more pensioners to remain in the workforce at least part-time, and is likely to some extent to put more pressure on available jobs.

Nevertheless, in January 1978 the House of Commons did receive a petition signed by one million people demanding that the Government allow everyone—both men and women—to retire at 60 if they so chose, on the grounds that the present distinction between the sexes "lacked reason and compassion."[14] Such a change is unlikely to be imminent since it was estimated in 1978 that the Government would have lost about £2,500 millions of its revenue if it had made the move then and at the same time maintained pensions at a rate which allows for annual adjustments to counter inflation. Since 1.4 million men would have been involved and, as well as paying for their pensions, the Government would have lost both the tax and national insurance contributions they pay, to maintain Government revenue through taxes would have required an increase in income tax of between 5p and 6p.[15] Private pension schemes would also have been hit, and, taking the average firm, it has been suggested that the impact of early retirement could virtually double present contributions.[16]

But again some countries have attempted to lower the age of retirement. In Belgium, as a response to youth employment, men at 60 and women at 55 employed in firms with 20 or more workers have the right to retire on special pre-pension payments of about 80 per cent of their normal wages. If employees exercise this right the employer is then obliged to take on an equivalent number of young people aged under 30.[17] In Denmark there are plans to encourage voluntary early retirement for workers over 60. It is estimated that for every 1,000 older workers who leave, 750 job openings will be created for young people.[18]

Certainly, in the UK, earlier retirement would seem to be abetted by many white collar employers: a recent survey by the Department of Employment's Unit for Manpower Studies showed there is a strong resistance to employing people over 50.[19] Less than a quarter of employers of the 7,500 white collar vacancies notified to Professional and Executive Recruitement were prepared to consider appointing an applicant over this age, one of the main reasons being that employers hoped recruits would make their careers with them and so concentrated on younger people.[20]

Of course not everyone wants to leave work. In 1977, for instance, British Post Office workers voted in favour of a resolution which would allow them to continue in employment until they were 65 if they so wished.[21] There is always a slight jump in the number of deaths in the two years or so after retirement, and, in the USA, partly in consequence of this, there has similarly been pressure to lengthen the time that people can stay at work.[22] Clearly, the psychological effects of the overnight change from being a "worker" to being a "pensioner", the incidence of which would increase if the average age of retirement were to drop substantially, merit additional study.

Job-sharing is an option less frequently considered than earlier retirement, but this has been practised for some years in academic institutions in the USA, and among both academic and some managerial staff in Sweden.[23] In Britain there are people who share clerical and administrative jobs in banks and insurance companies, local authorities and a few other places. However, the cut in pay and holidays for the employee and the increased costs to the employer of two sets of tax and insurance commonly make this an unattractive option.

Longer holidays, more sabbaticals and more education and training, like the 35-hour week, are all beset by the question of finance, and there will be heated argument about the manner in which the costs they bring should be met. But, whatever the difficulties, unless the alternative of accepting a permanently high level of unemployment is chosen, one combination or another of these different work sharing schemes seems destined to become the rule rather than the exception in future employment in the UK.

Financing New Employment: the Conservative view

Whether or not work sharing becomes an important element in employment creation, a considerable volume of funds would be required for any large scale generation of new jobs. In recent years there has been no shortage of suggested ways in which jobs might be created. Greater public expenditure, the stimulation of the private sector, selective import controls and sterling depreciation all have their advocates. But, while this debate can still be pursued, the June 1979 Budget has now clearly identified the direction in which the Conservative Government, with its large parliamentary majority, intends to proceed.

The policies of the Government were always likely to reflect in large part the views of Sir Keith Joseph, one of the Conservative Party's most prominent economic policy makers. It is his expressed opinion that "Government cannot create effort or enterprise or high productivity but it can create a framework which encourages people, in their own interest, to be enterprising and effective workers."[24] He argues that if private enterprise is allowed to flourish the labour market will prove capable of continuing to absorb the vast numbers it has done since World War Two. He blames a combination of government over-spending, over-taxing, over-borrowing and over-regulating for destroying jobs and preventing even more coming into existence than have been preserved by job protection. In his view, the fear that technological advance will cause increased unemployment might well prove ground-less since, though the history of the last 200 years has been "packed with labour saving inventions", this has only contributed to a seemingly limitless demand for varying combinations of goods, services and voluntary leisure.[25]

In order to stimulate market mechanisms and increase demand, Joseph has consistently advocated policies which reduce taxation and which would, he feels, have the effect of encouraging entrepreneurs to set up small firms, so generating new employment. Such policies should be accompanied by other measures designed to increase the flexibility and mobility of labour by devoting more money to training and re-training and by increasing the pay and status of managers, engineers, and skilled workers.

Not long before the May 1979 General Election in the UK a Conservative Party Study Group report similarly highlighted the need for expenditure on training programmes and proposed a universal training and opportunities scheme for all 16 to 18 year-olds not in full time education.[26] All those who enrolled for courses would be regarded as workers in training and would be paid an allowance "akin to the £19.50 allowance given under the Youth Opportunities Programme."[27] The net cost was put as high as £700 millions a year. Although it did not claim to represent official Conservative Party policy, the report carried a foreword written by two current Cabinet Ministers, Jim Prior and Norman St John Stevas, in which they claimed the document "undoubtedy constitutes an outline charter for youth."[28]

On the question of technological innovations in microelectronics the Conservative Party has appeared both bold and confident. To ensure that Britain does not fall behind in the application of micro-processors *and thus jeopardise jobs*, Norman Lamont, Under-Secretary of State for Energy, has argued that nationalised industries (the Post Office in particular) should encourage technological change through their ordering policy.[29] This theme was expanded in a discussion paper from the Conservative Computer Forum[39] which suggested that, since the State in all its forms (local government, nationalised industries etc) controls over half of Britain's wealth and over a third of all equipment purchases, the UK Government should place development contracts, including commitment to bulk purchase, with at least two suppliers of new technological equipment in order to meet the specified future needs of the public sector. The paper went further by proposing that the Government take the lead in erecting a "Buy European" framework for all public sector purchases within the EEC, mirroring the highly effective "Buy American" legislation of the United States.

The Computer Forum report conceded that even after Conservative policies "have created a climate in which change can take place, in which small businesses can grow large, in which established businesses will create jobs in their competition to win Government development contracts and exploit the spin off", it would still be a decade before the situation is "sufficiently improved".[31] In the meantime, it argued, publicly financed schemes to create short or long term jobs — such as in reclaiming the city centres or nursing the mentally sick — should be introduced. "The objective of any Government", it stated, "should be to gainfully employ the unemployed, either in public works or in looking after the elderly and ill, or to retrain them: not to waste their time with make-believe or idleness."[32] For such pre-election sentiments as these to be given substance an increase in public expenditure would undoubtedly have been required.

In the same month that the Conservative Computer Forum put the case for greater government intervention in job creation, Jim Prior, now Secretary of State for Employment, stressed that changes in the nature and structure of employment wrought by technological innovations might require fundamental changes in our whole attitude to work. The "work ethic", he concluded, would itself have to be brought into question.[33] The following week, immediately before the General Election which was to bring the Conservatives to power, Peter Walker, now Minister for Agriculture, speaking at the European Computer Review, put the case even more strongly. Those in his party, he argued, who relied on market forces to implement the new technology were inviting disaster. "The political system has got to organise technical change in a civilised way . . . There is a need to develop a rational approach to employment and unemployment acceptable to the nation. On current performance we will have 20 per cent unemployed by the mid-1980s through new technologies and trading patterns, and that is unacceptable."[34]

Before the Budget proposals there were thus within the Conservative party—as within other parties—markedly dissenting opinions. But, these notwithstanding, the broadly accepted and basic Conservative approach remained one of cutting public expenditure and taxes in order to encourage growth and greater wealth creation in the private sector, which was itself expected (or hoped) to enable unemployment to be reduced.

This approach to the management of the British economy was the foundation on which the first Budget of the new Conservative Government was built. Sir Geoffrey Howe, clearly articulating many of the views previously expressed by the Prime Minister and Sir Keith Joseph, introduced an undisguised monetarist budget with a reduced target range for money supply, a reduced public sector borrowing requirement and public spending cuts of £1,500 millions for 1979. Industry support was cut by £210 millions; employment programmes (including retraining) by £170 millions; expenditure on energy by £320 millions; spending on State education by £55 millions; education aid programmes by £50 millions; and Department of the Environment expenditure by £440 millions. The Rate Support Grant given to local authorities was reduced by £335 millions, and there are also hidden cuts, for instance in health service expenditure, caused by the maintenance of cash limits which take no account of rising prices.[35]

At the same time there was a significant switch from direct to indirect taxation. The thresholds at which income taxes become payable were raised and income taxes were cut across the board (albeit with considerably smaller tax reductions being granted to the lower paid than to the higher: the basic rate was cut from 33 to 30 per cent, and the top rate from 83 to 60 per cent). With candour the Chancellor explained that such reductions in income tax would enable people to pay the higher prices resulting from a massive increase in value added tax and hence in the prices of goods which (unlike, for example, food and children's clothing) were not zero-rated. VAT was increased from a standard rate of 8 to 15 per cent.

Excise duty on petrol was increased, and it was announced that sales of public assets (including more of the State's holdings in British Petroleum) would provide £1,000 millions to fund the Government's deficit. Restrictions on outward flows of capital were relaxed, allowing greater investment by UK firms overseas. Encouragement was given to small businesses, which were permitted to write off the deferred tax liabilities arising from earlier stock relief; and the profit limits within which the small companies rate of corporation tax of 42 per cent became payable were also raised to a new lower limit of £60,000 and an upper one of £100,000. However, while the Chancellor's strategy was clearly to encourage investment, in one important respect he was unable to be consistent in his budgetary proposals: the Minimum Lending Rate was raised from 12 to 14 per cent, which was bound to mean that for many borrowers (not least small companies) the bank lending rate would be in the region of 17 or 18 per cent. Mortgage interest rates were expected to show consequent rises.

Immediate reaction to the Budget was predictably mixed. It was certainly regarded as radical in the proper sense of the word; but many (not least among them Mr Callaghan, the former Prime Minister and now Leader of the Opposition) predicted a stormy winter of wage demands. It was inconceivable to most commentators that trades unions would do other than attempt to keep wages in step with prices (which themselves would rise sharply with VAT increases), whatever extra part of their earnings union members might now keep rather than surrender in taxes.[36]

Nevertheless, the Government has remained, at least in public, firmly of the opinion that in the medium and long term the only way to "squeeze inflation out of the system" and at the same time to create jobs is to encourage private investment. Explaining the need to reduce the Public Sector Borrowing Requirement in order for it to be compatible with monetary targets, the Chancellor in his Budget speech affirmed that, "We need to rely less on curbing the private sector, and put more emphasis on fiscal restraint and economy by the public sector." Higher public sector borrowing, argued Sir Geoffrey, would only make things worse. "In the end," he said, "we should have less growth, less employment and even higher inflation."[37]

But, in the beginning (though this was not made so explicit) there will anyway be less growth, less employment and even higher inflation, unless and until the changes which the Government has predicted in private investment and private job creation come to pass. The Treasury's own economic forecast for the next 12 months, published at the same time as the Budget proposals,[38] was that the whole British economy would shrink by one per cent; industrial production would drop by 2.5 per cent; government spending on goods and services would be reduced by 2.5 per cent; investment in the public sector would drop by 4.5 per cent; and investment in the private sector would also fall, by 0.5 per cent. Both exports and imports were expected to grow, by 5.5 and one per cent respectively; and inflation from the third quarter of 1978 to the third quarter of 1979 was anticipated to be at a rate of 16 per cent, and for the subsequent 12 months at 13.5 per cent.

However, according to a report in *The Observer*[39] published just five days after the Budget, other Treasury forecasts were even more dire. In the report, Adam Raphael and William Keegan claimed that predictions of two million (registered) unemployed and of inflation reaching 20 per cent were suppressed because of their acute political sensitivity. A good deal of credence had already been lent to these predictions the day after the Budget when Patrick Jenkin, the Secretary of State for Social Services, disclosed that inflation in the 12 months ending in November 1979 was actually expected to be 17.5 per cent[40] (there also being a possible margin of error of a further two per cent). If wage settlements do in fact prove to be in line with price rises and the Government maintains its tight control of money supply, large numbers of bankruptcies (caused by rising staff, materials and borrowing costs) and even greater unemployment will be inevitable.

Financing New Employment: the Labour view

The question, then, is not so much whether in the short term economic difficulties will increase, or would anyway have done so under Labour, but whether in the long term things will improve.

In the view expressed by many in the Labour Party and the trades unions long before the Conservative Government's cuts in public expenditure, reliance cannot be placed on the private sector to generate adequate investment and employment opportunities in what is a harsh economic climate. Specifically, it is argued by critics of the Government's proposals that tax cuts have a much less significant effect on employment levels than do increases in public expenditure.

Stuart Holland, formerly at Sussex University and now a Labour MP, has used the Treasury's model of the economy to show that reflation through public spending could create up to six times more jobs over a year than reflation through equivalent tax cuts.[41] He also maintains that this major difference in potential job creation is accompanied by negligible differences in the money supply and the balance of payments. In discussing the manner in which the required increase in public spending might be funded, Holland and his collaborator, Paul Ormerod, have cited the National Institute's Economic Review of February 1977, which assessed the extent to which the money would anyway be recouped from tax paid by newly employed workers and from reduced expenditure on unemployment benefits. If in 1977 200,000 jobs were to have been created by £1,000 millions of public spending, this would have resulted—assuming an average wage of about £70 per week and the standard and marginal tax rates then in operation—in a tax clawback of about £250 millions. A further £250 millions would have been saved on unemployment and supplementary benefits; and about £50 millions would—before recent large increases in VAT—have come from the indirect taxation of additional consumption. Allowing for a margin of error, the figures indicate that half the initial expenditure would have been reclaimed. Holland claims that the Treasury's own model shows that, in such an exercise, after two years some £665 millions would be recouped, leaving £335 millions of the £1,000 millions of public expenditure to be found elsewhere.[42]

For Holland, big business is an obvious target as a source of finance for the increase in public investment. In real terms, he argues, the profits of all industrial and commercial companies rose by only seven per cent between 1970 and 1976, while the profits of the top 25 UK companies increased by 70 per cent over the same period. Though big business was undoubtedly affected by the post-1974 crisis, its real profits nevertheless increased 10 times as much as did those of the manufacturing sector as a whole.[43]

One conclusion of recent researches on the British tax system[44] is that the effect of the range of rebates allowed to business (including relief on stock appreciation, the 1973-75 liability for which can now, since the June 1979 Budget, be written off)[45] has been effectively "to eliminate the corporation tax liability of UK manufacturing industry." Though the profits of big business have risen in absolute and relative terms since 1969, Government revenue from corporation tax (which remained largely unaffected by the June 1979 Budget) plummeted from £1,322 millions in 1969 to £178 millions in 1976.[46] The top 20 industrial firms, which between them showed profits in 1976 of £4,323 millions, paid a total of only £145 millions in tax in 1977.[47] (In that year, British Petroleum, Esso, Rio Tinto Zinc, Courtaulds, Grand Metropolitan, GKN, Dunlop, Reed International, Bowater and Ford paid no corporation tax at all.) Had corporation tax been paid at near the nominal rate of 52 per cent then £2,000 millions more tax would have been raised from those 20 companies alone.[48] The most recent (Labour Government) White Paper on government expenditure plans included an estimate, albeit a "particularly tentative" one, that the tax revenue foregone from companies for 1978-79, through capital allowances, stock reliefs, reduced rates for small companies etc, amounted to £6,100 millions.[49]

Holland dismisses as discredited the claim that when public investment is reduced, private investment increases commensurate with the reduction. In practice, between 1975-6 and 1978-9, private sector investment only grew from 8.8 to 9.4 per cent of total national expenditure: a rise of £1,300 millions in contrast with a fall in public sector investment of £4,700 millions.[50] Furthermore, after the Labour Government's cuts in public expenditure, the investment intentions survey made by the Department of Industry predicted a marked decline in the growth in manufacturing industry during 1979 and an actual fall in 1980;[51] and, after the Conservative Budget, total private investment was still expected to fall.[52] The increase in unemployment resulting from the public sector cuts of the former Labour Government was, according to the Treasury's model, 600,000 over the three years, 1976-78.[53] Neither Ministers nor the Treasury have made public anticipated increases in unemployment as a direct result of Conservative public sector cuts.

Like Holland, the former Labour Secretary of State for Energy, Tony Benn, is also convinced that the unemployment problem can only be tackled through increased public spending in the form of investment for the fulfilment of social needs: "Only public expenditure can convert human needs into economic demands able to command resources and help restore full employment."[54] Before the General Election, Benn drew a parallel between what he perceived as the need for more public expenditure and the way in which the unemployment problems of the 1930s were resolved by rearmament.[55] Expenditure on arms proved an effective way of creating jobs and it revitalised the shipyards in the Clyde and the engineering factories in the Midlands. Benn feels that the challenge of this generation is to find a way of getting back to full employment without rearmament and war. His answer would be to use public expenditure to convert social needs into effective demands for better schools, educational facilities and hospitals and an improved built environment.

One possible source of revenue for increased public expenditure is, it has been claimed, North Sea oil. David Basnett of the GMWU, and Vice-Chairman of the Trades Union Congress, has argued that this "windfall" provides the United Kingdom with an opportunity to alleviate, or at least to offset, the anticipated reduction in employment opportunities.[56]

In 1977 the National Institute's Economic Review estimated that, given the continuance of the then policies, the short-term cumulative benefit of North Sea oil and gas from 1978 to 1981 would be £34.5 billions in terms of balance of payments improvement, and £14 billions in terms of public sector revenues.[57] Another estimate put the Government's annual revenue at £4.6 billions by 1985.[58] Basnett has voiced the opinion that much of the income from oil should be used directly or indirectly to generate employment and to finance the spread of employment across the community. He is prepared to concede that it is necessary to revive the competitiveness of British manufacturing industry and that this would require "a substantial proportion of North Sea revenues", but has stressed that concomitant employment creation effects would be minimal, if not negative, in many sectors. He has also acknowledged that substantial resources would need to be invested in energy and energy saving. But, in Basnett's view, the remainder of the Government's oil income should be used directly to finance investment and current expenditures in the public services, particularly in education, training and health. This he regards not only as a desirable end in itself but as a means by which significant permanent employment could be generated.

Basnett underlines the conclusion that the creation of additional jobs by public service current spending is by far the cheapest method of raising employment levels, and he has argued that this could be achieved by the use of oil revenue without massive detrimental effects on the balance of payments and on the public sector borrowing requirement.[59] However, Basnett considers that on its own even this approach would be enough neither to offset the effects of the continuing growth in the potential workforce nor meaningfully to reduce existing levels of unemployment. He feels that it must be accompanied by a reduction in the length of the working year in order to share out those jobs available, and that the most effective way of doing this is to shorten the working week. A cut in basic hours to 35 a week, on the assumption that only 40 per cent of the net reduction would actually be translated into additional demand for labour, would, in his opinion, create about 400,000 to 500,000 jobs.[60]

Basnett recognises that the shorter week will result in a rise in costs, but rejects the Government and CBI view that any reduction has to be self-financing since he feels that this, in effect, is to say that it cannot be employment-creating. For him, the immediate cost impact is not as important as the balance of costs. It must be seen against the enormous costs already being incurred by the Treasury, by the economy as a whole and by the 1.46 million people currently unemployed. Louie Burghes and Frank Field have pointed out[61] that the opportunity cost of loss in national income caused by high and rising levels of unemployment is enormous. While it should be recognised that in any such calculation effective demand for the goods and services which could have been provided must be assumed, they have calculated that in 1974 unemployment resulted in a loss of output of £1.2 billions. In 1975 the figure rose to £5.7 billions, and in 1977 to £8 billions. If the fall in tax revenue and in contributions to the national insurance fund, and the increase in payments of social security benefits and claims on the redundancy payments fund, are added in, then the total cost to the community of running the economy at a high level of unemployment for the period 1974-77 they estimate to have been £20 billions.[62]

Though considerations of international competitiveness might otherwise dictate that a shorter working week cannot occur in Britain alone, Basnett regards North Sea revenues as putting the United Kingdom in the advantageous position of being able to bear the costs of promoting job creation linked to work sharing in the public sector and of switching job creation subsidies to employers introducing work sharing schemes. Only by these sorts of measures does he think the gloomy projections of up to four million unemployed in the UK[63] by the end of the century could be proved wrong.

In the light of opinions such as these, it is not surprising that the Conservative Budget—which took quite the opposite course—should have been greeted by the Labour Party and trades union leaders with widespread disapproval. Mr Callaghan deemed the Budget a reckless gamble with Britain's economic future. "I do not have confidence," he declared, "that his (the Chancellor's) prescription, his keystone in policy, a reduction in taxation, is going to achieve all these wonderful benefits that he is outlining to us."[64]

In contrast to the reaction of Sir John Methven, director-general of the Confederation of British Industry ("The new package," he predicted, "will help to put Britain back on its feet again by restoring incentives all the way from the shop floor to the boardroom."),[65] the response of leading trades unionists was far from encouraging. The general secretary of the TUC, Len Murray, declared that "The Budget gives no confidence that the Government wants a working understanding with the trade union movement in the interests of the British people as a whole",[66] and David Basnett again attempted to bring to public attention the fact that the unemployment to which the Budget would give rise was destined to be made even worse by the energy crisis and the use of microchip technology.[67]

Since the Budget, similar misgivings have accompanied the announcement of each measure to reduce public expenditure, and it is clear that — as well as there being profound ideological differences between the unions' leadership and the Government — there is also genuine distrust felt by a great many commentators of the efficacy of the Conservative "solution" to Britain's economic ills. Understandably, of immediate concern to protagonist and antagonist alike is the effect in the short term (not least on employment levels) of tight control of money supply, expenditure cuts and rising prices. There is, however, a real danger that Britain's political leaders, seduced by the urgency of the present debate, will fail to recognise the context in which it is being engaged. Such recognition is vital. There is every indication that, unless far-reaching decisions are taken now about the future role in our society of work itself, the transition to a new and more automated age will cause as much disruption of Biritish homes and families as did the stormy marriage of coal and iron a century before.

6 The challenge to be met

The process of formulating policies by which to transform what will otherwise be a series of severe industrial and employment discontinuities into an orderly transition is certain to generate intense argument over the direction in which to proceed. Political recriminations can cloud political judgement, and to some extent are bound to in debates which will inevitably be dominated by ideological rather than practical considerations of the role of public versus private ownership and control. Yet, whatever grand design is to be pursued (and the Government has made clear the route it wishes to follow), certain immediate obstacles can be recognised and must be negotiated. The political, economic and social consequences of rapidly increasing unemployment might well demand, if not a change of course, then at least a change of tack; and the whole question of employment raises a number of matters on which in today's economic and industrial climate a judicious government would be wise to pay attention to its critics.

The basic argument remains one of whether the required massive improvements in job availability (and in the equity with which jobs are available) will in fact be realised in the medium and long term solely by encouraging enterprise and high productivity.

While enterprise, increased productivity and greater competitiveness are all eminently desirable in British industry (and declared intentions to stimulate them are welcome) there is little indication that even an invigorated British economy will spawn sufficient jobs to achieve acceptable levels of employment. The first reason is that money foregone in tax and hence withheld from public investment has not in the past been matched by equivalent private investment.[1] Second, even if it were, private investment to maximise productivity and profits (which is the perfectly legitimate aim of investors) will not necessarily result in increased employment. As the capabilities of microelectronic technology are beginning to teach us, there is little direct, and sometimes even an inverse, correlation between productivity (especially when measured in terms of output per man year) and employment. It would be imprudent to espouse the view of Sir Keith Joseph that such technological innovations are destined to have little adverse effect on jobs[2] in what, with a growing potential labour force, is anyway a worsening employment situation. Unemployment will be the bane of the Conservative Government unless its longer term plans to encourage greater private generation of wealth actually work; unless they result in a wide distribution of the benefits they bring; and unless they are anyway accompanied by programmes to mitigate the immediate effects of their implementation.

There has, therefore, to be a greater measure of direct involvement in planning for employment than the Government has so far indicated is likely. Though short term job creation cannot be expected to answer long term employment problems, the maintenance (and perhaps restoration) of job creation programmes—none of which was wholly abandoned in the Budget, but all of which were cut back—should form part of this planning. The fact that further applications for support from the Manpower Services Commission have already been halted and the MSC has been required to prune its operations by £110 millions[3] will enable the Government fully to assess the merits of the programmes as they were, and now are, operating. With only six weeks in office before the presentation of its first Budget, the Government is likely to have had too little time to conduct such an appraisal, and, indeed, to examine the present and potential importance of job creation schemes at a time when local authorities have also had their rate support grant cut by £335 millions.[4] It will prove a costly decision—and one which in all probability will later have to be reversed—if the Secretary of State for Employment is obliged (in direct contradiction of the views he and his Cabinet colleague, Peter Walker, have expressed) to dismantle important retraining and employment creating programmes to achieve relatively small savings in public expenditure.

Leaving aside, for the moment, their long term impact, advances in microelectronics have already introduced a new dimension to the problem of redundancies, and one which the Government will have to consider. In order to predict and to respond to imminent changes it is vital to monitor—hopefully with the cooperation of industry and unions—the numbers and types of jobs affected.[5] At the very least this is important to a determination of the emphasis which should be placed on the retraining of workers. Specifically, the Training Opportunities Programme of the Manpower Services Commission was one element of employment expenditure which was cut back by the Budget. Before it suffers further pruning its real value in achieving greater flexibility and mobility of the workforce (goals the importance of which has been stressed by all Conservative industry and employment spokesmen) should be carefully reassessed.

Arguments to restore reductions in the money allocated to employment provision (like those to limit redundancies throughout the public sector) can, of course, be expected to cut little ice with a government pledged to reduce public expenditure, and especially with one which is determined to redeem such pledges without delay. Certainly any sizable addition to the public sector borrowing requirement, which has so recently been reduced from £9,250 millions to £8,250 millions for the current year,[6] is unlikely to gain support from the Conservative benches. Nevertheless, with unemployment figures rising, in part as a direct consequence of the Budget, it would prove valuable for the Government itself to examine both the real costs (after allowance is made for savings in social security payments and for tax and national insurance clawbacks) of job provision and protection by or in the public sector, and of ways in which such an operation could be made as cost-effective as it can be in creating long term employment opportunities. The incentive to work will have little real effect unless sufficient work is available, and it will not be. At present on average there are in the UK 43 people actually seeking unskilled labour for every such job there is available (and in parts of Merseyside, it has been claimed, a staggering 409 unskilled job-hunters per job[7]), so the problem is not simply a lack of desire or incentive to work, but rather a lack of work to be found. Faith in the long term benefits of reduced public expenditure is bound to remain a fundamental tenet of the present Government. But such faith in the future cannot afford to be blind to problems of the present.

Whatever jobs can be created to limit the growth of unemployment in the short term, they will not be sufficient to stem anticipated rises in unemployment which will result from more school-leavers joining the workforce. If unemployment is in anyway to be contained, the shorter working week and greater equity in the sharing of available work will need—together with short term job creation—to form a part of government policy.

The opposition of the Confederation of British Industry to the shorter week is understandable, as will be union claims for compensation for the reductions in overtime which, if it is to succeed, will have to accompany the move. But the Government should nevertheless agree in principle to a 35-hour week, the hours to be allocated in such a way as to create new employment opportunities, and should establish the machinery whereby problems attendant on its introduction in both public and private sectors can be minimised. The task will not be an easy one, and it is one which, without comprises on all sides, will prove incapable of performance. It nonetheless remains one on which consensus must be achieved.

The costs incurred by the establishment of a shorter working week, as with those of job creation generally, will have to be met from somewhere. If they are not to be imposed directly on employers (and by them passed on to consumers), they will have to be paid out of public funds and hence raised in taxes. It has been argued that more money would be available for the employment of people to provide for social needs if large UK corporations were required to pay corporation tax.[8] Thanks to three main tax reliefs—deductible interest charges, free depreciation and stock appreciation relief—Britain's largest firms have recently almost entirely avoided paying the tax, whereas medium-size companies with smaller overseas operations (allowing them less freedom to make use of agreements by which they avoid paying taxes both overseas and at home) have carried a heavier tax burden. The argument that the estimated £6.1 billions of revenue foregone in 1978-79 through these reliefs and reduced rates for small companies should not be foregone in the future is clearly worthy of examination. Indeed it was recognised by the Meade Committee that there might be merit if, instead of attempting to assess what part of profits should be taxed, companies were taxed on cash flow, the taxable amount being simply the difference between money received by the company from the sale of plant, goods and services and the money spent on the same.[9]

However, it would be wrong to conclude that since some companies have avoided corporation tax, they pay no tax at all: industrial and commercial rates, together with employers' National Insurance sur-charges, at present bring in an annual amount similar to the £6.1 billions figure.[10] It would also be wrong to think that the extra corporation tax which would be required to be paid would not ultimately come from individuals in the form of shareholders (including those reliant on pension funds), who could expect smaller dividends, and consumers, who could expect higher prices. Since, by raising the amount from companies rather than via personal income taxes, the bulk of increased costs are likely to be passed to the consumer, such a move would be consistent with a desire to tax consumption rather than earnings. On balance the Government should therefore decide whether it wishes itself to determine the manner in which the more than £6 billions a year should be spent, and—if so—whether it should be devoted to investment designed to ease present and anticipated employment problems.

In making these decisions, the Government will of course have to consider whether, if companies were obliged actually to pay the full rate of corporation tax, there would be a flight of investment capital from Britain to countries with lower taxes. In this context it is worth noting that, in the developed world, all OECD countries are grappling with high levels of structural unemployment and with youth unemployment in particular, and all have increased public expenditure on a variety of job creation schemes.[11] If these countries fail in their efforts to secure greater employment opportunities for their citizens, their failure will not result solely in more money having to be devoted to the welfare of a growing number of unemployed. It will also damage national economies by reducing consumers' effective demands — the "aggregate demand" — for the goods their industries provide. The larger the pool of unemployed and the lower their purchasing power then the greater will be the adverse effect of reduced consumption of both home-made and imported goods. Cooperation between countries is therefore required: and, significantly, the EEC is reported to be considering ways of generating public investment in jobs and preventing firms moving from country to country in search of the lowest taxation by standardising corporation tax throughout the community.[12]

All the above responses should be examined without delay since a programme of action is urgently required. But in the 1980s and 1990s the employment situation can be expected to change so radically that it will demand the introduction of measures of an entirely different magnitude.

At present in the UK there are roughly two million people unemployed.[13] By 1990 — without taking the effect of microelectronics into account at all — the number could well be five millions.[14] By the end of the century, in the absence of significant changes in the way in which work is allocated, increased automation is likely to have raised the number of jobs required (in addition to those we have at present) to something considerably higher than that.

Of course, the existence of microelectronic capabilities does not mean that these will be exploited fully and quickly by British industry. A study by the Science Policy Research Unit[15] has shown that British manufacturing firms still find it difficult to recruit sufficient engineers to get the best out of the present generation of machine tools. As P. Senker of SPRU has observed, "Microelectronics based numerically controlled machine tools are likely to require even higher levels of expertise in order to exploit their productive potential";[16] and, in the wider context, "British industry has a long history of failing to take full advantage of the opportunities presented by technical change for creating wealth and employment."[17] But, at whatever rate advantage is taken of opportunities to create wealth, the acknowledged trend is for the application of microelectronics not to create accompanying employment but instead to render more and more jobs redundant.

While it is exceedingly difficult to quantify the jobs which are likely to be lost, Clive Jenkins and Barrie Sherman, basing their estimates on a paper presented by the ASTMS to the Trades Union Congress, have attempted a sector by sector breakdown of anticipated job losses in the short, medium and long term.[18] Their findings are given in the Table. They expect long term reductions (after 25 years) in the number of jobs to total 5.2 millions: no less than 23.2 per cent of their original sample labour force. By the end of 1983, 4.6 per cent of the jobs of the original

Table: ESTIMATED EMPLOYMENT TOTALS BY INDUSTRIAL SECTOR, IN THOUSANDS OF WORKERS.

	Present	Short term (5 years)	Medium term (15 years)	Long term (25 years)
Agriculture, Forestry and Fishing	357.3	340	300	300
Mining and Quarrying	341.7	310	280	250
Food, Drink and Tobacco	688.7	630	500	450
Coal and Petroleum Products	36.9	35	30	25
Chemical and Allied	428.6	430	390	360
Metal Manufacture	469.7	450	350	250
Mechanical Engineering	928.1	920	800	620
Instrument Engineering	148.3	130	100	80
Electrical Engineering	741.4	700	520	410
Shipbuilding and Marine	174.7	170	120	80
Vehicles	786.6	750	500	400
Metal Goods	535.5	540	500	430
Textiles	468.3	430	300	120
Leather and Fur	40.4	40	38	35
Clothing and Footwear	365.3	350	260	220
Bricks, Pottery, Glass and Cement	261.3	260	240	190
Timber and Furniture	258.7	255	250	220
Paper, Printing and Publishing	536.2	500	350	250
Other Manufacturing	325.5	310	300	400
Construction	1215.5	1200	1000	1000
Gas, Electricity and Water	339.1	340	350	350
Transport and Communications	1413.8	1300	1000	1000
Distributive Trades	2657.1	2550	2000	1600
Insurance, Banking and Finance	1136.6	1050	780	650
Professional and Scientific	3589.3	3650	3500	3650
Public Administration	1872.1	1600	1700	1800
Miscellaneous Services	2249	2100	2100	2000

Source: Clive Jenkins and Barrie Sherman, *The Collapse of Work,* Eyre Methuen, 1979.

workforce will already have disappeared, and ten years later 17 per cent will have gone. The challenge, then, is not just to react astutely to worsening unemployment in the next few years, but—by formulating appropriate policies now—to achieve an orderly transition to an era in which there will be substantially reduced opportunities for conventionally paid employment.

In their recent book, *The Collapse of Work,*[19] Jenkins and Sherman are confident of the direction in which the future is to be sought. There is a need, they claim, to shift the whole ethos of society away from conventional, paid employment: 'We do not believe that work *per se* is necessary to human survival or self esteem. The fact that it appears to be so is a function of two centuries of propoganda and an educational system which maintained the "idea" of work as its main objective, but which singularly failed to teach about leisure and how to use it.'[20] In their future society they see a smaller workforce producing, by the exploitation of new technological capabilities, sufficient wealth to provide dramatically increased redundancy pay, payment for the unemployed, early pensions and school attendance grants. Financial security will be afforded those who, for any period of time or after retirement, are no longer in the paid workforce. Employment will be generated in this prosperous climate by meeting the basic needs of health, education, social welfare, care for the elderly, public transport and housing. Small firms will be encouraged. Leisure industries can be expected to grow (providing products like gardening and sports equipment, and services like those of hotels, restaurants and cafes) and employment will be generated for actors and other entertainers. Life-long education will be important not only for its own sake, but also in helping people to adapt to changes in their careers. As Professor Stonier of Bradford University has argued,[21] society will require an increasingly versatile labour force to respond to the needs of a rapidly changing economy in which people in the course of a working lifetime will commonly have two or three careers. A major shift towards knowledge-based industries is anticipated, which will require longer periods of education interspersed with paid employment, and new forms of education with new curricula. These themselves will constitute important social and cultural changes in the conduct of society.

In the view of Jenkins and Sherman the way to achieve these benefits is through the immediate acceptance and exploitation of technological innovations. They recognise that in the short term this will create unemployment, the effects of which will have to be mitigated by appropriate governmental policies. But, they explain, in their view of the future, "Technological unemployment will be based on high growth, high profits and returns, a highly competitive manufacturing and service base and high incomes, and these enable constructive policies to be adequately funded."[22]

However, in the opinion of the present authors, there is little guarantee — even with support for the microelectronic package coming from unions, management, Government and Opposition — that high growth and profits will be achieved. (Neither — and here we agree with

Jenkins and Sherman—is there any indication that high profits, if they were to be made by the labours of those remaining within the workforce, would by some means or another be fairly distributed throughout the whole population.)

The reason for our comparitive pessimism is simple: the acquisition by British industry of the benefits which microelectronic technology will bestow will not grant the UK a competitive edge over her rivals when their industries have benefited from the same increase in technological capabilities. In the application of microelectronics the USA is far ahead of the UK; and, while the fact that the British economy is uncompetitive (and with low productivity and a high exchange rate is getting more so) is more significant than government expenditure on research and development, it should be remembered that the governments of Japan, France and the FGR have already granted their own microelectronics industries considerable support to the tune of roughly £500 millions, £270 millions and £250 millions respectively.[23] Neither are these the only rivals in the field. The outlook for world trade is far from encouraging, and the effect of further rises in oil prices will make a bad situation worse.

More likely than the Jenkins-Sherman future is one in which there is little or no economic growth and the people of the UK are divided into those who number in their households at least one paid worker and those who, because they do not, are largely reliant on whatever unemployment compensation it is decided they should receive. For as long as people in the latter group are adequately provided for, society will continue to function in much the same way as it does today. If their economic conditions compared with those of people in paid employment are allowed to worsen and their numbers to increase, considerable internal strife could ensue. It is unlikely in the Western democracies that unemployment can continue to grow without an unidentifiable threshold level of joblessness being reached at which social disruption and unrest will threaten the stability of national economies.[24] As an EEC official has observed, "Everyone knows that youth unemployment is the biggest powder keg in European politics. What we are all wondering is how long is the safety fuse."[25]

This is not the future which the present authors would choose, but we have a duty to stress that the risk is a real one, and one which cannot be dismissed as extraneous to economic planning. Simple truths cannot be escaped. During periods of some, if not high, economic growth it is possible, without the rich being impoverished, for poorer sections of society to be afforded greater benefits than the more affluent. However, in periods of little or no growth this cannot be achieved. In such a situation the poor, whose numbers could increase with rising unemployment, can benefit neither in absolute nor in relative terms without a transfer of resources, or of the opportunity to secure a greater share of resources through paid employment. Without such a transfer the gap will widen between the rich and the poor, between the paid and the compensated, and the dissatisfaction and impatience of the latter will grow. It is as dangerous for advocates of the free market economy to discount the political and social implications of rising unemployment as it is foolish for their antagonists to dismiss the importance of profitable industrial activity in providing wealth, the benefits of which all governments (of whatever hue) have long considered it their responsibility more equitably to distribute.

We would urge therefore that the measures described in this paper by which to come to grips with the immediate problems of increasing unemployment and to ensure greater equity in the sharing of available work receive consideration. The shorter working week, work sharing and job creation through the provision of social needs merit urgent examination. Their implementation might at least allow time for the formulation of policies appropriate to a longer term future in which our present attitudes to work and to management of the economy will have undergone a more fundamental revision than in any period since the Industrial Revolution.

Notes

Introduction

1. Colin Hines, *The Chips are Down*. London, Earth Resources Research, 1978.

1   The Response of Government

1. The silicon chip or microchip is a miniature integrated electric circuit with many different components like transistors and resistors etched onto a wafer of silicon crystal. The microprocessor is one type of chip which can be programmed in many different ways and can carry out the computing functions of a computer. In addition to microprocessors there are memory chips, which store data and programmes, and input-output chips which allow the user to communicate with the microprocessor. See the preliminary table in *The New Technology*. Counter Information Services Anti-Report No 23, (1978) undated.

2. Peter Laurie, "Britain Takes a Silicon Gamble" in *New Scientist*, 15 February 1979.

3. *Ibid.*

4. John Elliott and John Lloyd, "Scheme to meet challenge" in *Financial Times*, 7 December 1978.

5. Peter Large, "Chip talking at the polytechnic for more than 1,000 engineers", *The Guardian*, 18 July 1979.

6. Advisory Council for Applied Research and Development, *The Applications of Semi-Conductor Technology*, HMSO, September 1978.

7. *Ibid.* p28.

8. When introducing the three-year, five-point programme for microelectronics devised by the Departments of Industry, Employment and Education and Science, Mr Callaghan, while admitting there would be "crucial job losses" stressed that there would also be new jobs created. John Elliott and John Lloyd, *op. cit.* See also Joan Gray, "UK's salvation is in micro revolution, Jim tells TUC", *Electronics Times*, 25 January 1979.

9. Malcolm Peltu, 'Minister optimistic on jobs — but it's an "act of faith"' in *Computer Weekly*, 12 October 1978.

10. Arthur Smith, "Jobs risks denied by Varley", *Financial Times*, 5 December 1978. Mr Varley claimed that microelectronic technology "can generate as many new jobs as it displaces."

11. Speaking at the opening of the British Computer Society's 1979 Conference, Lord Peart is quoted as saying that if Britain adopted the new technology as fast as its competitors the number of jobs created would outweigh those lost. Paul Taylor, 'Microchip transition "urgent"' in *Financial Times*, 5 January 1979.

12. In his address to a Bow Group meeting in August 1978, for instance, Sir Keith Joseph dismissed as groundless fears that technical advance could be expected to create unemployment. Rupert Cornwell, 'Labour's policies "destroying jobs"', *Financial Times*, 25 August 1978.

13. Central Policy Review Staff, "Social and Employment Implications of Microelectronics", Mimeo, November 1978.

14. *Ibid.* pp4-5.

15. Malcolm Peltu, "The 1980s—A Decade of Technological Advance", paper in Proceedings of National Conference on Planning for Automation, 17 January 1979, held at Polytechnic of the South Bank, Mimeo.
16. Central Policy Review Staff, *op. cit.* p7.
17. Personal communication from Peter Bennett of ASTMS.
18. APEX, 'APEX Response to CPRS Report "The Social and Employment Implications of Microelectronics".' Typescript, January 1979, p3.
19. *Ibid.* p3.
20. *Ibid.* p2.
21. Central Policy Review Staff, *op. cit.* p19.
22. Quoted by Tom Forester, "Society with chips and without jobs", *New Society,* 16 November 1978, p387.
23. *Ibid.* pp387-388.
24. In his speech of 24 August 1978 to the Bow Group, Sir Keith Joseph argued that there was a limitless demand for goods, services and leisure and that the labour market, if allowed to by government policies, could absorb vast numbers. See Rupert Cornwell, *op. cit.*
25. Iann Barron and Ray Curnow, *The Future with Microelectronics,* Frances Pinter, 1979, p199.
26. *The Strategic Impact of Intelligent Electronics in the US and Western Europe 1977-1987,* Arthur D. Little Consultancy, reported by Peter Large, "Million new jobs from chips", *The Guardian,* 20 March 1979.
27. This is an estimate of the relative costs of an integrated circuit today and 15 years ago. ASTMS Discussion Document, "Technological Change and Collective Bargaining", Mimeo, (1978) undated, p7.
28. Malcolm Peltu, *op. cit.*
29. *Ibid.* p10.
30. Quoted by Malcolm Peltu, *ibid.* p11.
31. *Ibid.* p11.
32. This was published in book form more than a year later as *The Future with Microelectronics,* Iann Barron and Ray Curnow, *op. cit.*
33. *Ibid.* p13.
34. *Ibid.* p227.
35. Simon Nora and Alain Minc, *L'informatisation de la société,* Documentation Française, Paris, May 1978.
36. The wording is that of a French correspondent of *New Scientist,* "The next French revolution", 8 June 1978.

2 Unemployment and the Effects of Microelectronics

1. This is the July 1979 figure of registered unemployed in the UK.
2. Barrie Sherman, "Unemployment and Technology", paper presented to CAITS Alternatives to Employment Conference, Mimeo, 18 November 1978, p2
3. In 1978-79 a total of 190,000 were taken off the unemployment register by the Youth Opportunities and Special Temporary Employment Programmes and the Community Industry scheme. MSC, *Annual Report,* 1979.
4. Manpower Services Commission, *Review and Plan,* 1978, para 216.
5. *Department of Employment Gazette,* April 1978.
6. Professor C. Freeman, J. D. Bernal Memorial Lecture, Birkbeck College, 23 May 1978.
7. These figures are given in CAITS, "The Future of Employment in Engineering and Manufacturing", Mimeo, (1978) undated, p24, quoting *The Times,* 24 June 1978.

8. Philip Sadler, "Technology and the future of employment in Europe", *Technology Choice and the Future of Work*, Symposium Proceedings, British Assoc. for the Advancement of Science, November 1978, p71, Table IV.
9. *Ibid.* p70, Table III.
10. *Ibid.* p71.
11. Jay Gershuny, *After Industrial Society? The Emerging Self-Service Economy*, London, Macmillan, 1978.
12. Howard Rush, "Automation and Employment", paper presented to BA Conference on Automation, Univ. of Swansea, April 1978, Mimeo, SPRU.
13. CAITS, *op. cit.* p22.
14. *Ibid.* p22 puts the number of jobs required to reduce unemployment to 500,000 by 1981 at two millions. See also Job Gap Curve in MSC, *Review and Plan*, 1977, HMSO, p21.
15. ASTMS Discussion Document, "Technological Change and Collective Bargaining", Mimeo, (1978) undated, p22.
16. *Ibid.* p22.
17. *Ibid.* p22.
18. Quoted in Butler Cox Foundation, *Trends in Office Automation Techniques*, Report Series No 4, December 1977.
19. Special Report on word processing, *The Guardian*, 6 June 1978.
20. Butler Cox Foundation, *op. cit.*
21. APEX, *Office Technology: The Trade Union Response*, London, March 1978, p8.
22. *Ibid.* p8.
23. ASTMS, *op. cit.* p25.
24. APEX, *op. cit.* p7.
25. ASTMS, *op. cit.* p24.
26. *Ibid.* p24.
27. Counter Information Services, *The New Technology*, Anti-Report No 23, London, (1978) undated, p10.
28. Personal communication from Peter Bennett of ASTMS.
29. Jane Barker and Hazel Downing, "Office Automation: Word Processing and the Transformation of Patriarchal Relations", paper presented to Conference of Socialist Economists' Microelectronics Group, Mimeo, January 1979.
30. David Dangelmayer, "The job-killers of Germany" in *New Scientist*, 8 June 1978.
31. Simon Nora and Alain Minc. *L'informatisation de la société*, Documentation Française, Paris, May 1978.
32. Personal communication from Malcolm Peltu.
33. ASTMS, *op. cit.* p26.
34. *Ibid.* p26.
35. *Ibid.* p26.
36. "Some 30 per cent of all mail traffic is inter-company . . . A further 40 per cent of mail traffic flows from business to household, and 15 per cent from household to business." Iann Barron and Ray Curnow, *The Future with Microelectronics*, Frances Pinter, 1979, p150.
37. *Ibid.* p26.
38. The foregoing examples are given in Counter Information Services, *op. cit.* p11; and Jane Barker and Hazel Downing, *op. cit.* p18.
39. ASTMS, *op. cit.* p22.
40. Barrie Sherman, *op. cit.* p4.
41. Calculated from ASTMS, *op. cit.* p35.
42. Quoted by Alec Hartley, "New technology could put 5M out of work", *The Guardian*, 12 May 1978.

43. Reported in *Computer Weekly*, 19 January 1978.
44. *Ibid.*
45. ASTMS, *op. cit.* p28, based on New Earnings Survey 1977.
46. G. Coulouris, I. Page and T. Walsby, *The Potential for Integrated Office Information Systems*, Butler Cox and Partners Ltd, December 1977.
47. APEX, *op. cit.* p12.
48. *Ibid.* p12.
49. *Ibid.* p11.
50. *Ibid.* p19.
51. *Ibid.* p17.
52. The manager was Hugh Jenkins, Director General of Superannuation Investment for the Coal Board. Reported in "Institutional Investment and the Inner City", *Estates Gazette*, 25 November 1978.
53. Reported by Alec Hartley, *op. cit.*
54. National Electronics Council, "Report on the Social and Economic Impact of the Use of On-Line Computers in Manufacturing Industry", November 1977.
55. ASTMS, *op. cit.* p20. See J. M. McClean and H. J. Rush, "The Impact of Microelectronics on the UK", SPRU Occasional Paper No 7, June 1978.
56. ASTMS, *op. cit.* p20.
57. *Financial Times*, 2 August 1978.
58. Speech by Ken Corfield, President of the Telecommunications Engineering and Manufacturing Association to the Royal Society, 10 March 1977.
59. *Ibid.* Quoted by David Fishlock in *Financial Times*, 16 March 1977.
60. Reported in *Financial Times*, 11 March 1977.
61. ASTMS, *op. cit.* p14.
62. *Ibid,* p14.
63. Keith Dickson and John Marsh, "The Microelectronics Revolution: A Brief Assessment of the Industrial Impact", Occasional Paper, Technology Policy Unit, Univ. of Aston, December 1978, p50.
64. Reported in *The Engineer*, 20 July 1978.
65. *Ibid.* 23 February 1978.
66. ASTMS, *op. cit.* p16, quoting *The Engineer*, 23 February 1978.
67. Reported in *The Engineer*, 21 July 1977 and 3 November 1977.
68. Reported in *The Economist*, 10 June 1978.
69. E. Braun, "The Challenge of Automation in the Manufacturing Industry", Occasional Paper, Technology Policy Unit, Univ. of Aston, 1978.
70. ASTMS, *op. cit.* p16.
71. Keith Dickson and John Marsh, *op. cit.* p50.
72. Robin Wood, "Spray unit could guide UK car makers out of mist", *Electronic Times*, 31 May 1979.
73. E. Braun, *op. cit.*
74. Keith Dickson and John Marsh, *op. cit.* p27.
75. ASTMS, *op. cit.* p20, citing *The Engineer*, 20 January 1977.
76. ASTMS, *op. cit.* p11, citing an advertisement for the Design Engineering Show, National Exhibition Centre, Birmingham, 4-8 December 1978.
77. International Metalworkers Federation Report of Activities to 24th World Congress, Munich, 24-28 October 1978, p230.
78. Barrie Sherman, *op. cit.* p4.
79. ASTMS, *op. cit.* p11 referring to a report in the *Electronics Times*, 9 November 1978.
80. Calculated from table given in *Financial Times*, 1 February 1978.
81. Michael Parkin, "Thorn to cut 1,000 more jobs", *The Guardian*, 7 May 1978.

82. John Ardill, "TV firm to cut 2,200 jobs", *The Guardian,* 6 April 1978.
83. Personal communication from Julius Marstrand.
84. Arthur D. Little study, *op. cit.* cited by Joan Gray, "Will robots be slain by intelligent electronics?", *Electronics Times,* 1 February 1979.
85. Manpower Services Commission, *Training For Skills,* 1977, Annex 4.
86. "Dial-a-repair saves the spectrometer service engineer", *New Scientist,* 29 June 1978.
87. ASTMS, *op. cit.* pp42-43, citing report in *Financial Times,* 24 August 1978.
88. This was argued by Mike George, "Which Future and Whose Future in Manufacturing Industry in the UK", paper presented to CAITS Alternatives to Employment Conference, Mimeo, 18 November 1978, p3.
89. Health and Safety Executive, *Shift Work and Health: A Critical Review of the Literature,* HMSO, 1978, reported by David Fishlock, 'Shift work risks "exaggerated" ', *Financial Times,* 13 December 1978.
90. Lucas Aerospace Combine Shop Stewards Committee, "Implications of the Corporate Plan", paper presented to the CAITS Alternatives to Employment Conference, Mimeo, 18 November 1978, p11.
91. *Shiftwork,* pamphlet by BSSRS, 1978.
92. Marie Jahoda, "The Impact of Unemployment in the 1930s and the 1970s", SPRU, Mimeo, C. S. Myers lecture, March 1979, quoted in Howard Rush, *op. cit.*
93. Research of Prof. Harvey Brenner of Johns Hopkins Univ. cited in Howard Rush, *op cit.*
94. This was calculated by Prof. Brenner's team and included in the World in Action programme, *The Reckoning,* broadcast on 5 February 1979.

3 Methods of Reducing Unemployment

1. *The Times,* 27 September 1976, quoted in Frank Field (Ed), *The Conscript Army,* London, Routledge and Kegan Paul, 1977, p141.
2. *The Times,* 9 December 1976, quoted in Frank Field (Ed), *op. cit.* pp141-142.
3. John Cunningham, "The massive price of fending off unemployment", *The Guardian,* 26 April 1978.
4. John Cunningham, *op. cit.*
5. *Ibid.*
6. John Palmer, "Their future behind them?" *The Guardian,* 17 October 1977.
7. Martin Loney, "Manpower Services Commission—An Ill-considered Response", paper presented to Conference of the Assoc. of Community Workers, Typescript, September 1978.
8. *Ibid.*
9. David Hencke, "Young blacks to get training priority", *The Guardian, 9 March 1978, quoting Mr Douglas Knight of the MSC.*
10. *Ibid.*
11. For instance by Martin Loney, *op. cit.*
12. *Ibid.* pp2-3.
13. John Cunningham, *op. cit.*
14. Martin Loney, *op. cit.* quoting the Holland report.
15. These and subsequent figures are taken from the Budget speech of Sir Geoffrey Howe (and accompanying documents), published on 12 June 1979 and reported the following day.
16. Reported by David Hencke, "Prior orders new job scheme cuts", *The Guardian,* 27 July 1979.
17. *Ibid.*

72

18. Richard Norton-Taylor, "Whitehall leaks inquiry urged", *The Guardian*, 30 July 1979.
19. Simon Watt, "Adventures in the Informal Sector", paper presented to CAITS Alternatives to Employment Conference, Mimeo, 18 November 1978, p3.
20. These figures are given in "The young and out of work", *Department of Employment Gazette*, August 1978.
21. This is the conclusion of a study by Prognos AG European Centre for Applied Economic Research, Basle. Reported by John Wicks, "12m jobless forecast for Europe", *Financial Times*, 29 December 1978.
22. Robert Taylor, "The threatened eclipse of the Rising Sun", *The Observer*, 21 January 1979.
23. *Ibid.*
24. *Ibid.*
25. ILO, "How the West Fights Unemployment", *ILO Information*, Vol 14 No 4, 1978.
26. John Palmer, *op. cit.*
27. These examples are quoted in ILO, *op. cit.*
28. OECD, "What are OECD Countries Doing?", *OECD Observer*, January 1978.
29. David L. Birch, *The Job Generation Process*, report published by Massachusetts Institute of Technology, 1979. Reviewed by Nigel Hawkes in *The Observer*, 22 April 1979.
30. David L. Birch, *op. cit.*
31. ILO, *op. cit.*

4 Production for Social Needs

1. The Cambridge Economic Policy Group in *Economic Policy Review*, March 1978, put estimated unemployment by 1990 at 4.6 millions, and this assumed a three per cent growth rate to 1980 (which has not been achieved), and subsequently a two per cent rate declining to zero towards the end of the decade.
2. Prominent among them have been Tony Benn and David Basnett. See also James Robertson, "Master or servant? Which role for technology in post-industrial society?", *Technology Choice and the Future of Work*, Symposium Proceedings, British Assoc. for the Advancement of Science, November 1978.
3. Batelle Memorial Institute, "The Potential for Substituting Manpower for Energy", Social Affairs Division of the Commission of the European Communities, July 1977. See also Christine Thomas, *Material Gains*, London, Earth Resources Research, 1978.
4. Batelle, *op. cit.* quoted in Mike George, "Which Future and Whose Future in Manufacturing Industry in the UK?", paper presented to CAITS Alternatives to Employment Conference, Mimeo, 18 November 1978, p7.
5. Batelle, *op. cit.* cited in CAITS, "The Future of Employment in Engineering and Manufacturing", Mimeo, (1978) undated, p5.
6. "At its peak the group employed 18,000 workers. The workforce has now been reduced to 12,000 with further cuts planned." From Joan Gray, "Swords into ploughshares just won't go", *Electronics Times*, 12 April 1979.
7. Lucas Aerospace Combine Shop Stewards Committee, "Corporate Plan—An alternative contingency strategy to recession and redundancies", 1976.
8. Lucas Aerospace Combine Shop Stewards Committee, "Implications of the Corporate Plan", paper presented to the CAITS Alternatives to Employment Conference, Mimeo, 18 November 1978, p3.
9. LACSSC, 1978, *op. cit.* p6.
10. Phil Asquith, "Worker's Control or Control of the Workers?", Science for People, No 42, Summer 1979, p11.

11. Joan Gray, *op. cit.*
12. *Ibid.* Alan Witney, Lucas Aerospace personnel director is quoted as saying, "Experience tells us we'll come unstuck if we try to compete outside aerospace."
13. Gerald Leach *et al, A Low Energy Strategy for the United Kingdom,* London, Science Reviews, 1979.
14. *Ibid.* p19.
15. CAITS, *op. cit.* p45.
16. *Ibid.* p45.
17. See, for instance, David Elliott, "Energy Options and Employment", Mimeo, CAITS, 1979, Table 26, p104.
18. For a discussion of combined heat and power, energy options and their social implications, see also Graham Searle, *Energy* in the "Towards a New Political Agenda" series, London, Liberal Publications Dept. 1977; and Walter C. Patterson, *The Fissile Society,* London, Earth Resources Research, 1977.
19. In June 1979 it was reported that the combined heat and power group of the Department of Energy had presented to the Secretary of State a report urging greater use of CHP. David Hencke, 'Use of power station "waste heat" urged', *The Guardian,* 25 June 1979.
20. Gerald Leach *et al, op. cit.* p27.
21. *Ibid.* p27. Overall energy utilisation of about 70 per cent is twice that of the best electricity generating station.
22. David Elliott, "Can Alternative Technology Create Jobs?", paper presented to CAITS Conference on Alternatives to Employment, Mimeo, 18 November 1978, p4.
23. Gerald Leach *et al, op. cit.*
24. Quoted in David Elliott, 1979, *op. cit.* p19.
25. Frederic Romig and Gerald Leach "Energy Conservation in UK Dwellings: Domestic Sector Survey and Insulation", IIED, Mimeo, June 1977; and Gerald Leach *et al, op. cit.*
26. David Elliott, 1979, *op. cit.* p19. Here he follows Godfrey Boyle, "Let's have some more radioactivity", *Undercurrents,* No 15, 1976.
27. UK-ISES, *Solar Energy — A UK Assessment,* Royal Institution, London, 1976.
28. Cited by David Elliott, 1978, *op. cit.* p20. For official view see Dept. of Energy, *Solar Energy: Its potential contribution within the United Kingdom,* Energy Paper 16, HMSO, 1976.
29. "Jobs from the Sun", California Public Policy Centre, 1978, quoted in David Elliott, 1978, *op. cit.* p5.
30. Quoted in David Elliott, 1978, *op. cit.* p2.
31. "Jobs from the Sun", quoted in David Elliott, 1978, *op. cit.* p2.
32. LACSSC, *op. cit.*
33. Mike Cooley, "New technologies: whose right to choose?", *Technology Choice and the Future of Work,* Symposium Proceedings, British Assoc. for the Advancement of Science, November 1978.
34. David Elliott, 1979, *op. cit.*
35. David Elliott, 1979, *op. cit.* pp4 and 107, argues that 660,000 man years of work could result from the nuclear power programme achieving 40GW capacity, but that 25GW is more likely, with 400,000 man years of work materialising. He concedes that in Energy Commission Paper 18, "Manpower requirements for the energy industries", Dept. of Employment, 1978, the figures given for work creation are 900,000 and 600,000 respectively.

36. David Elliott, 1979, *op. cit.* assumes a 36-37 mtce contribution from solar, wind, wave and tidal energy, but Energy Commission Paper 1, "Working document on energy policy", Dept. of Energy, 1977, p45, estimates the likely actual contribution to be 10 mtce.
37. Gerald Leach *et al, op. cit.*
38. LACSSC, 1978, *op. cit.* p10.
39. *Ibid.* p10.
40. *Ibid.* p11.
41. John Darwin and Hilary Wainwright, "Generalising the Lucas initiative: a movement for workers' plans?", paper presented to CAITS Conference on Alternatives to Employment, Mimeo, 18 November 1978, p8.
42. *Ibid.* p8.
43. *Ibid.* p8.
44. These examples were quoted by John Darwin and Hilary Wainwright, *op. cit.* p3.
45. For a brief account of the whole process see Nicholas Falk, "Getting Small Enterprises Started" Appendix B: Telegraph Textiles Case Study, paper present to CAITS Alternatives to Employment Conference, Mimeo, 18 November 1978.
46. *Ibid.* Appendix B.
47. At the time of writing the precise nature of the cut-backs in the operations of the MSC were not known, but an internal document prepared by the Commission at the request of the Secretary of State for Employment had indicated sizable reductions in the Training Opportunities Programme. David Hencke, "Prior orders new job scheme cuts", *The Guardian,* 27 July 1979.
48. *Community Work Service,* No. 15, London Community Work Service, May 1979.
49. This is the theme of "Lewisham—An Approach to an Employment Policy", a discussion paper prepared by the staff of Voluntary Action Lewisham and The Albany, Mimeo, revised May 1979.
50. Reported by David Hencke, "Heseltine warns councils not to flout £440 million cuts", *The Guardian,* 13 June 1979.
51. £233 millions is to be cut by 1982-83. Jane McLoughlin, "Industry aid to be cut by £233M", *The Guardian,* 18 July 1979.
52. Alan Burkitt, "Tameside—hoping to ease the fears", *Electronics Times,* 2 November 1978.
53. Hertfordshire County Council Planning Dept., "Monitoring Issue Report: Micro-electronics and Structure Planning in Hertfordshire", Mimeo, January 1979.

5 Work sharing and Job creation

1. *Department of Employment Gazette,* April 1978.
2. Christian Tyler, "Postal engineers end action on winning 37½-hour week", *Financial Times,* 18 September 1978.
3. *TUC Annual Economic Review,* 1978 put job creation at more than 700,000 with a 35-hour week and a marginal increase in overtime working. It was estimated that this would give a 6-8 per cent increase in crude labour costs. Quoted in CAITS, "The Future of Employment in Engineering and Manufacturing", Mimeo, (1978) undated, p43.
4. Clive Jenkins and Barrie Sherman, *The Collapse of Work,* Eyre Methuen, 1979, p154.
5. *Ibid.* p165.
6. Moss Evans, general secretary of TGWU, put it succinctly: "Employers and Government must be convinced that we are determined to bargain for a shorter working week without loss of pay." Quoted in 'Shorter hours "key to unemployment bogey"', *The Guardian,* 7 September 1978.

7. CBI, *Britain Means Business*, September 1978.
8. Kenneth Gooding, "Free industry and prosper—CBI", *Financial Times*, 8 September 1978; and Robert Taylor, "CBI is to fight 35-hour week", *The Observer*, 10 September 1978, quoting CBI, *op cit.*
9. Tom Stonier, "Materials production labour requirement in the post-industrial society", working paper commissioned by Central Policy Review Staff, Mimeo, 10 November 1978. See also *British Labour Statistics Yearbook 1979*, HMSO, Table 43.
10. John Palmer, "Shorter working week mooted", *The Guardian*, 22 March 1978.
11. John Palmer, *op. cit.*
12. From Reuter in Paris, "European workers protest against rising unemployment", *The Guardian*, 6 April 1979.
13. John Palmer, *op. cit.*
14. Tom Tickell, "Cost of leaving", *The Guardian*, 25 February, 1978.
15. *Ibid.*
16. *Ibid.*
17. "Special Employment and Training Measures", *Department of Employment Gazette*, February 1978, p165.
18. ILO, "How the West Fights Unemployment", *ILO Information*, Vol 14 No 4, 1978.
19. Alan Pike, 'Employers "not keen" on taking over-50s', *Financial Times*, 4 January 1979.
20. *Ibid.*
21. Tom Tickell, *op. cit.*
22. *Ibid.*
23. Adrienne Boyle, "Share a Job?", North Lewisham Law Centre, Mimeo, (1978) undated.
24. Mick McLean, "Climate of enterprise is needed, says Sir Keith", *Electronics Times*, 4 January 1979.
25. Rupert Cornwell, 'Labour's policies "destroying jobs" ', *Financial Times*, 25 August 1978.
26. Reported by John Fairhall, "Tory call for £700M youth training scheme", *The Guardian*, 21 June 1978.
27. *Ibid.*
28. *Ibid.*
29. Reported by John Lloyd, "Tory micro-electronics policy", *Financial Times*, 8 December 1978.
30. Philip Virgo, "Cashing in on the Chips: A policy for Exploiting the Semiconductor Revolution", Conservative Computer Forum Discussion Paper, Mimeo, March 1979.
31. *Ibid.* p17.
32. *Ibid.* p17.
33. Peter Large, "Work ethic may be on way out, says Prior", *The Guardian*, 22 March 1979.
34. Robert Batt, "Micros open Tory gulf in market forces row", *Computing*, 5 April 1979.
35. Budget speech and accompanying documents published on 12 June 1979 and reported in the press on the following day.
36. This point was made by Mr Callaghan, Leader of the Opposition, in his reply to the Budget address. Reported in 'Unions "will not settle for less than rise in prices" ', *The Guardian*, 13 June 1979.
37. Budget speech reported with headline, "We must squeeze inflation out of the system", *The Guardian*, 13 June 1979.

38. "Treasury Year", *The Guardian*, 13 June 1979.
39. Adam Raphael and William Keegan, "2 million jobless report hushed-up", *The Observer*, 17 June 1979.
40. *Hansard*, Vol 968, No 16, Col 441.
41. Stuart Holland and Paul Ormerod, "Why we must increase public spending", *New Society*, 25 January 1979.
42. *Ibid.*
43. *Ibid.*
44. J. A. Kay and M. A. King, *The British Tax System*, Oxford University Press, 1978.
45. Budget announcement reported by Clive Woodcock, "Warm response for new incentives", *The Guardian*, 13 June 1979.
46. Stuart Holland and Paul Ormerod, *op. cit.*
47. *Ibid.* quoting J. A. Kay and M. A. King, *op. cit.*
48. *Ibid.* quoting J. A. Kay and M. A. King, *op. cit.*
49. *The Government's Expenditure Plans 1979-80 to 1982-83*, HMSO, 1979, quoted in Stuart Holland and Paul Ormerod, *op. cit.*
50. Stuart Holland and Paul Ormerod, *op. cit.*
51. *Ibid.*
52. For the twelve months from June 1979, Treasury forecasts estimated a drop of 0.5 per cent. "Treasury year", *The Guardian*, 13 June 1979.
53. Stuart Holland and Paul Ormerod, *op. cit.*
54. Quoted by Mick McLean, "Tony Benn—contemplating the division of the rewards of the micro revolution", *Electronics Times*, 15 February 1979.
55. Tony Benn, "Automation and Employment into the 1990s", paper in Proceedings of National Conference of Planning for Automation, 17 January, held at Polytechnic of the South Bank, Mimeo, pp6-7.
56. David Basnett, "North Sea Oil—A Chance to Tackle Unemployment", *Lloyds Bank Review*, No 130, October 1978.
57. *National Institute Economic Review*, November 1977, p20.
58. David Basnett, *op. cit.* p8.
59. *Ibid.* p10.
60. *Ibid.* p15.
61. Louie Burghes and Frank Field, "The cost of unemployment" in Frank Field (Ed), *The Conscript Army*, Routledge and Kegan Paul, 1977.
62. *Ibid.* p85.
63. David Basnett, *op. cit.* p16, speaks of 2-4 millions on the dole by the year 2000.
64. Reply to the Budget speech, "Unions will not settle for less than rise in prices", *The Guardian*, 13 June 1979.
65. Quoted by Jane McLoughlin, "BR feel fares can be held", *The Guardian*, 13 June 1979.
66. Quoted by Keith Harper, "Unions warn of fight on the Budget", *The Guardian*, 13 June 1979.
67. *Ibid.*

6 The Challenge to be Met

1. Stuart Holland and Paul Ormerod, "Why we must increase public spending", *New Society*, 25 January 1979.
2. Speech to the Bow Group. Reported by Rupert Cornwell. 'Labour's policies "destroying jobs"', *Financial Times*, 25 August 1978.
3. Budget speech and accompanying documents published on 12 June 1979 and reported in the press on the following day.

4. *Ibid.*
5. The Dept. of Industry, in its booklet *Microelectronics — The New Technology,* lists nearly one hundred fields in which microchips have readily identifiable applications.
6. Budget speech, 12 June 1979. It could be argued that the PSBR has been reduced by virtue of part of it being financed by the sale of public assets.
7. These figures were presented in the BBC Radio 4 programme, The World at One, 18 June 1979.
8. Stuart Holland and Paul Ormerod, *op. cit.*
9. *Structure and Reform of Direct Taxation,* Report of Committee chaired by Prof. J. E. Meade, HMSO, 1977.
10. Frances Cairncross, "The company tax game", *The Guardian,* 10 March 1979.
11. OECD, "What are OECD countries doing?", *OECD Observer,* January 1978.
12. Reported by Barrie Sherman of the ASTMS in a reply to a question at the National Conference: Planning for Automation, held at the Polytechnic of the South Bank, London, 17 January 1979.
13. This is the round figure arrived at by adding estimated unregistered unemployment to the registered unemployed.
14. The Cambridge Economic Policy Group, in *Economic Policy* Review, March 1978, put estimated unemployment by 1990 at 4.6 millions, and this assumed a three per cent growth rate to 1980, and subsequently a two per cent rate declining to zero towards the end of the decade.
15. Howard Rush, "Automation and Employment", paper presented to BA Conference on Automation, Mimeo, April 1979, p3.
16. P. Senker, "Implications of Microelectronic Technology for the British Economy", SPRU, Mimeo, March 1979, p11.
17. *Ibid.* p17.
18. Clive Jenkins and Barrie Sherman, *The Collapse of Work,* Eyre Methuen, 1979, pp116-123.
19. *Ibid.*
20. *Ibid.* p141.
21. Tom Stonier, "Materials production labour requirement in the post-industrial society", working paper commissioned by Central Policy Review Staff, Mimeo, 10 November 1978.
22. Clive Jenkins and Barrie Sherman, *op. cit.* p176.
23. Japan is reported to have spent £500 millions by the end of 1978, and France and the FGR each to have rolling programmes of about £60 millions per annum: Tom Forester, "The micro-electronic revolution", New Society, 9 November 1978. See also Chris Harman, *Is a machine after your job? SWP, (1978)* undated; and *The New Technology,* Counter Information Services Anti-Report No 23, (1978) undated.
24. There have been many reports of workers' action in response to rising unemployment. See, for instance, "European workers protest against rising unemployment", *The Guardian,* 6 April 1978; Walter Ellis, "Jobless concern in Bonn", *ibid.* 24 August 1977; "West Germany's 35 hours of reckoning", *ibid.* 29 November 1978; and, from France, "Steel protests turn violent", *Financial Times,* 31 January 1979.
25. Quoted by John Palmer, "Their future behind them?", *The Guardian,* 19 October 1977.